Pickled Herring and a Trip to Mars…

By Judith Quain and James Kahle

About the Authors

Inspired by fond memories of their grandparents' indomitable spirit and the impact they had on their own personal lives, James Kahle and Judith Quain write the story of two young Swedes who negotiate a new world with hearts and hands that shape everything they touch.

For our children
Finn, Jen, Gerald, Jorge and Chris
and
the many generations of grandchildren
of Nils and Linnea

With special thanks to Paul Quain

and Linnea Sauter

ONE

A Butterfly Flutters Its Wings

"Somewhere in the world, a butterfly will always flap its wings and thwart our age-old craving to predict -- our own future." John Lienhard.

A strange man—unshaven, rumpled with clothes in tatters—stood at the end of the dirt driveway. Linnea, who was sitting in the backyard watching her granddaughter chase butterflies in the summer sun, sensed that someone was there. When she turned to see who it was, she realized that he was one of the men who rode the freight trains looking for work— one of the many that got off at the end of Hessing Street where she lived. In spite of his shabby suit and dirty hands, she greeted him with a smile and said, "God middag."

It was 1942 and finally jobs were becoming available, as

America geared up for war. Linnea listened to him tell his story—one that she had heard many times before during the darkest days of the Depression when she had helped to feed men who got off the train to look for work. She knew he must be hungry, so she invited him in for something to eat.

Inside her kitchen, where she had often fed those in search of a meal, she sat him down, sliced some of the warm bread that she had baked that morning, and made coffee.

I'm glad to do at least something for him, Linnea thought...*I know how it feels to not have an idea of what tomorrow will bring! Thirty-two years ago I was standing on the dock in Goteborg, Sweden with just ten dollars in my pocket... ready to board a ship that would take me away from everything I knew.*

But soon her thoughts of lunch were interrupted by sounds of her granddaughter, "Yudy"—she never could pronounce her J's—coming up the back steps.

Carried away by her memories, she had forgotten the man in her kitchen! Quickly she moved down the stairs to warn her of the man sitting at the table before she reached the top of the steps. Catching her, she whispered in her ear, "Don't be afraid, the man in the kitchen is dirty but he is kind and very hungry. Go wash up...after he leaves we'll go bumming and visit Elsa. We'll take the Grand Avenue bus and stop along the way for some smoked herring and fresh bread…and after that we'll go to the racetrack!"

Early that morning, Linnea had decided to celebrate this anniversary of her arrival in America by having lunch with her friend, Elsa. For both of them, a visit was like going home. Even though Elsa was Danish, they spoke the same dialect. Blekinge, where Linnea grew up, was once a remote spot of the Kingdom of Denmark before it became a part of Sweden.

Linnea loved the horses. She didn't know much about the racing world but the exhilarating atmosphere of the track coupled with the beauty of such magnificent animals was always a thrill for her. An escape to the racetrack was a real treat and Linnea made the most of it while she was there. She didn't look at any racing forms, odds or the records of horses or jockeys…she just played her hunches. Her strategy was stress-free and very simple. One day it would be a hunch to make a bet on a grey horse or sometimes it was just a number that occurred to her—but she always came home with some, though not much, money in her pocket.

Meanwhile, the man in the kitchen had finished eating. Linnea gave him twenty-five cents and wished him well. Now, it was time to get "Yudybug" ready to take the bus.

Later that afternoon at the racetrack, a grey horse caught her attention, especially the number it was wearing. "Number seven," she said to Elsa, "this must be good luck…that's the day in June that I sailed to America!" As she walked to place a bet, her memories brought her back to that difficult time. *Leaving all that I knew was hard,* thought Linnea, *but Victor gave me courage…he seemed so sure it was the right thing to do.*

In 1906, her brother, Victor, was the first of the family to leave Sweden. Resigned to the unfortunate reality of his family's dire economic situation, he knew he needed to leave and that he might never return. Linnea felt the same once she had made her decision to leave. For her, there was no looking back. She was so excited about the prospects of the unknown adventure ahead that it was really all she could think about. She would miss her family and friends, but she also took solace in not having to endure the long dark and cold Swedish winters, the shortage of food, the monotonous routine of farm life and the confining self-imposed rules of the Lutheran religion. No matter what was ahead, she felt that it could not possibly be any worse than her present conditions. It was difficult to suppress the excitement she felt about her new adventure but, out of respect for her parents and siblings, she managed to keep her feelings in check right up until the day she left their tiny farmhouse.

She would never forget that day when she and Frida, her

younger sister began their long journey to America. Seated in the back of an open wooden wagon that was pulled by the neighbor's plow horse, they traveled the ten miles to the train station. Linnea tried to ignore the uncontrollable sobbing of her sister as they left their home, and passed the local church and some of their neighbors' farms for what would be the very last time. The slow pace of the horse-drawn cart prolonged the agony of her sister as images of their small home remained in view for what seemed to be an eternity.

Neighbors, who approached their wagon to say good-bye, wished them luck and offered food for the trip. Linnea wished she could put a whip to the horse so that her sister would not have to suffer such protracted separation pains. She never forgot how, from their position on the back of the wagon, they saw their present life slowly disappear from view. And how, with their backs to the driver, they couldn't see where they were going or what the future held for them as the horse continued his deliberate and slow pace towards the train station, where they would begin their journey.

On June 7, 1910, Linnea Alexia Cemalia Persson and her sister Alfrida were to sail to Boston on the S.S. Saxonia of the Cunard Line. In order to emigrate, they had obtained permission from the parish and the Assistant Vicar had issued them a Moving Certificate. It was a standard form with eighteen items to be filled out. It stated that they had been vaccinated, baptized and confirmed in the Church of Sweden, earned a passing grade in Christian knowledge and had partaken of Holy Communion in the Lutheran Church. Their emigration contract stated that the journey would be by steamer from Malmo, Sweden to Grimsby, England, then onto Hull and finally Liverpool by rail. From Liverpool they would sail to Boston. In all, the journey would take ten days. The cost was three hundred and eight kronor, or about ten dollars.

At the time, it was required that those immigrating to America have a sponsor in the USA. On the ship's manifest, she and her sister declared that they were headed for Victor's farm in Piper City, Illinois. Victor's letters had been full of enthusiasm for life in America. Piper City seemed far away to them then and they weren't sure that they could make it, but needed his name as a sponsor. Both young women, each with ten dollars and a small trunk holding all they owned, left their home in Morrum and traveled to Malmo to begin their journey to America. They entered "servant" as their occupation on the ship's manifest. At twenty-two, Linnea had some domestic skills, as did her sister, and had no doubt that they could find some work when they landed. Travelling by boat from Malmo to Hull, they boarded the train to Liverpool. There were so many Swedes getting on the train that Linnea took little notice of the handsome young man watching them as they boarded.

The young man, Nils Wansberg, was also headed for Liverpool and the S.S. Saxonia. His destination in America was North Cambridge, Massachusetts where he would meet his sister, Gerda, and her husband, Gustaf Frykberg. At twenty-four, Nils was an accomplished musician and skilled cabinetmaker. His dream was that these skills would be all he needed to start a life in America. With violin in hand and fifteen dollars in his pocket, Nils had left the Ervalla train station for the port of Goteborg, Sweden. From there he boarded the Algerie, a steamship ferry that would take him to Hull, England. A train would then take him from Hull to Liverpool where he would board the S.S. Saxonia.

On Tuesday morning June 7, 1910 Linnea and Alfrida walked down the gangway that led directly from their ship to the train of the Great Central Railroad that would take them to Liverpool. The dockside terminus, the Riverside Quay Railroad Station in Hull, was only four years old and had replaced the immigration waiting station that had served European immigrants for the last fifty years. The station was the culmination of improvements made in England over several years to accommodate the millions of European immigrants on their way to America via the steamships that left from Liverpool. The ability to board thousands of immigrants directly from arriving ships to waiting trains served to increase business for Britain's passenger ships and trains as well as to isolate immigrants from the general population. The vast majority of the European immigrants were poor, malnourished and, more importantly, potential carriers of disease. Cholera outbreaks in the past had been traced to the transient immigration population, and the health authorities pushed for the separation of immigrants from the general population to minimize possible contamination.

For Linnea and Frida, however, the process seemed like royal treatment as they conveniently transferred from boat to train in a matter of a few hours. Once on the railway station platform, their luggage was whisked away and placed on cars of the "The Great Central Railroad" train. This was only the second time Linnea had ever been on a train, and its length seemed never-ending to her.

True to British tradition, the train left precisely at 11:00 A.M. and would arrive in Liverpool some three to four hours later with stops in Leeds, Haddersfield, and Stalybridge. The railway system in England, bolstered by immigrant travel, was at its prime in 1910. The development of the steel industry during the latter half of the 19th century had rapidly replaced cast iron as the material of choice for locomotives. The engines were lighter, more flexible and a good deal more powerful which greatly reduced travel time for the steadily increasing passenger loads.

A light rain was falling when the train pulled out of the Hull station. Linnea pressed her face against the window so as not to miss a single moment of the trip. She was not disappointed. The trees, rolling hills, and even the architecture of the brick ivy-covered houses were excitingly different from rural Sweden. The constant chatter of fellow passengers who were speaking languages she had never heard before intrigued her. Thrilled to be in the company of such a variety of people, she was also excited by what they shared—a great adventure.

When the view of the landscape became repetitive, Linnea would pry herself from the window only long enough to engage one of her many fellow Swedes in conversation. Unabashed, she would tap them on the shoulder to ask… "What do you know about America? Do you have relatives there? Where in America will you be staying? Have you been there before? What is it like there?" It was only when her fellow passengers tired, that she would stop and return to her window.

Meanwhile, Linnea became aware that Frida didn't share her enthusiasm and their differences would last until they both arrived in Boston and beyond. Excited about the trip and all of the new surroundings, Linnea could barely keep still much less find the time to sleep. She couldn't understand how anyone could sleep at a time like this? *There would be plenty of time for rest*, she thought, *when they were aboard the Saxonia and the sun finally went down.*

Frida, on the other hand, was already homesick and uncomfortable with the strange food, gloomy weather, and travel in general. She was prone to cry easily and spent much of her time withdrawing into frequent naps. She hoped to wake-up to the familiar surroundings of her home in Sweden. But for Frida, the escape never lasted long. She would awaken only to tug on Linnea for comfort, as she attempted to deal with the reality of her situation. Linnea, who loved her younger sister and felt compassion for her plight, was becoming more and more annoyed as she felt Frida was robbing her of a precious once-in-a-lifetime view of a world she had longed to know. Nevertheless, her promise to her parents to take special care of her younger sister was an obligation that she was not going to dismiss lightly and Linnea dutifully did her best to console the despondent Frida.

As the train approached the outskirts of Liverpool, it was still raining but Linnea could see the outlines of the great steamships in the harbor that were waiting to take their eager passengers to America. She strained to see the lettering on the bow of each ship as she searched for the S.S. Saxonia. She remembered the literature describing the Saxonia and its distinctive tall single smoke stack, but it was still too gray and rainy to see clearly.

At 3:00 P.M. their train pulled into the docks at Liverpool. Once again there were dockside gangways, but this time they were leading up to the great ships from the train station platform. Collecting their luggage from the last car of the train, they began to walk along the dock, following the signs that designated the boarding location for their ship.

Saxonia at Liverpool   Copyright © Heritage Ships

It seemed like only moments ago that she was back in Sweden excitedly pouring over the Cunard Line brochures and envisioning herself on board. Nothing however, could have prepared her for the sight of the great ship that completely filled their view even from where they stood some one hundred meters away.

Whatever reservations she may have had about leaving her family or the fear of what lay ahead in America, these thoughts were put aside by the rush of excitement and anticipation of a seven day crossing of the Atlantic aboard the S.S. Saxonia.

TWO

A Story For Yudy

"There is a point at which everything becomes simple and there is no longer any question of choice, because all you have staked will be lost if you look back. Life's point of no return."
Dag Hammerskjold.

Lost in thought about their crossing to America, Linnea realized that she hadn't heard the phone ringing. Jumping up, she ran into the house to answer it. Linnea's daughter, Siri, was on the phone and wanted to know when she should pick up Judy. Linnea, who wanted to treat her granddaughter to a ride on the bus and a trip to see Elsa, told her that after supper would be soon enough. After she hung up, Linnea looked at the kitchen clock and realized that it was time to head for Grand Avenue to catch the bus.

On their way to Elsa's, they stopped by the Lithuanian Bakery and bought some bread. The loaves were so large that Linnea had to ask them to cut her just a pound of this dense dark bread, fresh with the aroma of caraway. A few steps down the street, they bought smoked herring and a tub of fresh sweet butter from the Swedish fishmonger.

By the time they arrived at Elsa's, they were hungry. Elsa embraced them both and urged them into the kitchen. While Elsa made coffee, Linnea chopped fresh chives and folded them into the creamy sweet butter. "Bug," as she sometimes called Judy, helped her spread the mixture on the still warm slices of bread.

"Now for the best part," Linnea said with a little laugh, "the fish!"

She unwrapped the glistening herring and couldn't wait to taste the tender flakes of this delicate fish that soon would meld with the sweet butter laced with chives. She knew that the first bite would give them—except Yudy who was always wary of eating fish—great pleasure. *Today is like going home,* Linnea thought...it *seems to be a day for memories.* She handed her granddaughter a plate and said, *"Varsågod."*

Judy had heard so much Swedish this morning and while she could only understand a few words, she was curious about this language and the country where her "Grammy" had lived.

Hoping for a story, she asked to hear about Sweden. She wondered what this land was like and was always curious if her Grammy missed it.

Too many questions, Linnea thought, *I don't want to go back there*. Thinking of those times always brought back contradictory feelings of nostalgia and pain, feelings she hadn't ever taken the time to sort out.

"Not now," Linnea answered, as she shook her head and screwed up her face as if she had just eaten something bitter. *Besides,* she thought, *Elsa had heard it all and neither one of them wanted to go back to those days.* But today, when she saw her granddaughter's disappointment, she thought, *Why not entertain "Bug" with a story of her past? Maybe even Elsa hadn't heard this one.*

Linnea laughed and began…"Everyday, I passed this big hotel in our small town of Ronneby. It was so beautiful and I always wondered what it looked like inside. One day, on my way into town to do some errands for my mother, I stopped along the way to pick some wildflowers by the hotel. It was called, The Ronneby Brunn…it was a grand spa that had visitors from all over the world. I loved to wander the walks and meadows around this great hotel and I always tried to peek into the gardens next to the house of the 'brunnsskänk', the person who gave the mineral water to the guests." Linnea then let out a laugh, slapped her knee and bent forward as if to tell Judy a secret. "But you know this day, I decided to do something different. I was so curious to see what it was like inside the hotel and, I thought…why not run into the hotel lobby for a quick look?"

"I had on a clean pinafore and hoped no one would notice that I wasn't one of the guests. Oh it was so beautiful… sweeping staircases, marble floors, and ladies sitting on fine furniture having tea. You should have seen it! I was so busy looking around that I didn't notice this lady who was watching me…and when the lady came up to me and asked me my name, I was really surprised and a little scared. I wasn't sure whether or not I was in trouble and so I said, Alfrida. It was my sister's name…it was the only name I could think of on the spot! I thought I was in trouble but then the woman surprised me and asked me if I would like to see more of the hotel. "

"I was so excited," Linnea went on, "And when we were walking around in the great rooms of this wonderful hotel the lady introduced herself as Sophia Andersdotter. She was the manager! Then she asked me to tea. Can you believe that…tea in this rich lady's salon? You know, that day changed my life. But let's eat now and then we can go catch the bus."

Linnea was relieved to end the story there. She knew that her granddaughter was too young to understand what it was really like back then and she couldn't possibly appreciate how delicious that hour in the spa's salon was to Linnea. For that moment in the spa, she forgot the cold dark mornings when she and her seven brothers and sisters got up and gathered around the fire before breakfast.

Yudy would never understand what those mornings were like, she thought...*knitting socks, sweaters, even underwear with her sisters before dawn while her brothers worked outdoors, then hauling water and scrubbing the wide pine floors to a gleaming white! By the time we left for school, my folks and the seven of us had been up for several hours!*

Linnea's parents had a tiny farm in Ronneby in the province of Blekinge. Nestled in the forests of Sweden's southernmost tip, Blekinge was known as the "the woodshed of Denmark." Due to its vulnerable position between Denmark and Sweden, the county was regarded as a buffer zone between the two countries. In the past, it was often the scene of clashes. Its towns and the countryside were burned and pillaged numerous times by Swedish and Danish troops alike until Blekinge became part of Sweden for good. Ronneby, where Linnea was born, was the oldest, but not necessarily the most prosperous town, in Blekinge. The town had a history of two hundred years of agony and despair in the form of wars, fires and the plague. It wasn't until the spa of Ronneby Brunn was established in the late 19th century that the town started to thrive. The hotel was a magnificent red and white wooden building, with towers and soaring spires, prize-winning gardens, sea baths and a mineral spring that showed an astounding percentage of iron. The spa became the largest in Sweden around the time Linnea's parents, Per Hakansson and Elin Persson, were married.

Toward the end of the century, Sweden was on its way to becoming a modern industrial nation. There was considerable urban settlement but there still were rural areas where small farmers and landless peasants were having a hard time making a living. The introduction of the smallpox vaccine and the fact that Sweden had been spared from war since 1814 had allowed the population to rise unabated—a phenomenon that the famous Swedish bishop and poet Esaias Tegne'r credited to "peace, vaccination and potatoes". As the population grew, farms that employed ninety percent of the working population became smaller, more fragmented and less productive. As a result, most Swedes had to eke out a living in agriculture with shrinking parcels of land and more mouths to feed.

Linnea remembered with bitterness those hard days when there was never enough, but she also had fond memories of the beauty of Blekinge. She often thought of the deep pine forests surrounding lakes of crystal clear water and the long coast with its numerous bays and beautiful views. No wonder that the Swedish word "bleke"—meaning "calm water"—was the name of the county.

Linnea often thought how such a small thing, like running into the spa that day, changed her life so much. That day opened her mind to all kinds of possibilities.

As it happened, Sophia Andersdotter, who was childless, was delighted to have the company of Linnea. In those days it was common for people of means to help in the support of a child from a poorer family with many children. Under these circumstances, she took Linnea under her wing and, for years, Linnea was introduced to the life of the wealthy in "Brunnspark." She watched them take their promenades through the magnificent gardens of this seaside resort that was resplendent with villas, tennis courts, cycle paths as well as the large elegant hotel. Linnea loved the sounds coming from the music room and found the lounge where they played cards and billiards to be the most exciting, especially when Mme. Anderdotter would give Linnea a portion of her winnings from the casino. Curious more than impressed, Linnea watched the idle rich play and took note of every detail. She knew that it was a life that she would never have and the stark contrast of the luxury of their lives to that of the common man in Sweden was offensive to Linnea's sense of fairness and equality.

But it was an opportunity for her to know a larger world, and when Sophia offered her a job that entailed doing errands and attending to her domestic needs, Linnea was grateful. "Brunnspark" had now become a fashionable seaside resort and Linnea was able to see a side of life that she knew she could never have. She heard the guests talk of New York and was fascinated by their descriptions. She listened incredulously as they spoke of "streets paved with gold"… "electric buses…the shopping on Fifth Avenue…mansions that covered a city block." Captivated by their talk and, curious as always, Linnea had decided on her eighteenth birthday that she would start to save for a trip to America.

Being surrounded by the wealth of the spa's patrons had made her all that much more realistic about what her opportunities would be if she were to stay in Sweden. Most of the guests were wealthy but the very poor patients—"the free drinkers"—were also able to enjoy the spa's mineral waters. Linnea was quick to notice that guests were put into different classes. The country people and the "free drinkers" were only allowed to drink the waters early in the morning before the well-to-do guests had arisen. Being at the spa heightened her awareness of the boundaries of her class and she realized that there wasn't much freedom to improve her situation. The government was conservative and the laws left little room for equal opportunity. Plus, she found the Lutheran church to be far too strict and didn't like the way it tried to legislate morality. Emigrating to America, she felt, would be a great opportunity to leave all this behind.

THREE

NILS

While Linnea and Judy were having lunch in Elsa's kitchen, Nils was hard at work when the noon whistle blew a loud blast and signaled the lunch break. As head carpenter in the Mars candy factory, he had spent the morning trying to come up with a better design for the production tables of the M&M line. The new candy-coated chocolates shipped out to the troops were becoming so popular at home that they were busy trying to keep up with the demand. As he ate his sandwich, Nils began to think of Linnea and the anniversary of their arrival in America. In spite of the noise in the plant and the work he had to do, he couldn't stop thinking about how much his life had changed.

It had been the right thing to do, he thought. *It wasn't anything like the trip that the earlier Swedish immigrants had*

... sailing on top of the cargo on freighters that had left Swedish harbors only to arrive in New York months later. There were so many stories of the many who didn't survive the trip and even if they did arrive, they were exhausted, half-starved, and then had to face another arduous journey to reach the Midwest. Steerage on the Saxonia was a luxury compared to those days.

Nils and Linnea had boarded the Saxonia on June 7th, 1910. The ship accommodated almost 2000 passengers and still maintained many of the luxuries found on the newer and larger Cunard Line ships. At a speed of fifteen knots, they made the trip from Liverpool England to Boston in just seven days.

Steerage passenger berths were little more than steel beds anchored to both the ceiling and floor. Although the men and women had separate quarters at opposite ends of the lower deck, their accommodations were similar. Each had four hundred sets of bunk beds in a large oak-floored room. There was only one four-drawer dresser for every ten bunk beds. Twenty people shared the dresser. It was reserved for some of their most personal effects such as razors, brushes, pictures etc., while the space below the lower bunk was used to store the bulk of their belongings. The lavatory facilities were adequate, but not private, and were located in a common area with open showers.

Nils was thinking how lucky he had been to find a lower bunk where he was able to store and keep a close eye on his violin. *I even found a dresser with two empty drawers,* he remembered.

Separating the men and women's dormitory areas was a lounge furnished with long wooden benches and small writing tables. Here passengers from a wide-array of nationalities in the steerage section could come together and share what they had left behind and why they were making the trip to America.

Nils smiled when he thought of his first impression of the lounge. *I couldn't help but pass my fingers over the wood of the furniture and railings when I walked through the lounge. To this day I'm still looking for imperfections in the finish of anything crafted in wood.* Nils had been a cabinet-maker and skilled carpenter in Sweden at a time when then, as now, materials and finish were prime concerns.

We always let the natural grain of the wood show through the stain…those benches and tables, he thought, *were so heavily varnished a dark color that it sucked the light out of this large room…it was so somber and heavy, it looked like a government waiting room!*

Nils smiled again, as he thought of how naïve he was back then…*Like the time I went up to what I didn't know was*

The Observation Deck. I remember pushing through some double swinging doors, going up a stairway and at the top of the stairs feeling a rush of warm salt air wafting through a door...I had found an open deck! I remember peering over the railing and seeing a gathering of several hundred people waving down below on the dock. I had figured they were waving to the first and second-class passengers standing on the upper decks above me. Even though I knew absolutely no one in the crowd below, I couldn't resist waving back. I guess I wasn't so stupid...your knee jerks in response to a doctor's well-placed tap with his hammer, you automatically say "you're welcome" when someone says thank you, you say "good morning" back when someone tells you good morning and you wave back when someone waves at you. I couldn't believe it...my arm suddenly shot up almost by reflex, and I waved back at the unknowns below! I was so caught up in the moment, with streamers and confetti thrown from the decks above, that I imagined that I was waving to my family and friends! I remember being so happy! It was then that I was sure that I had made the right decision to make this one-way trip.

When I returned to the lounge, I could hear the din of many languages—Polish, German, Norwegian and the two young women, whom I had noticed boarding the train for Hull speaking Swedish! Such excitement…but I couldn't place their accent!

During the 19th century the mountain ridges, general lack of adequate public transportation, and the rural makeup of Sweden isolated a number of regions from each other. This separation resulted in subtle but very discernable accent and intonation variations in the Swedish language. The differences could be compared to what an American from the Midwest would hear in traveling to Texas or some of the New England states.

But even from a distance, Nils thought, *I could see by the features of their faces and mannerisms that they must be related. Sisters or cousins, I guessed. I was struck by the good-natured personality of the taller of the two young women. She was having the time of her life! Laughing with her companion, this auburn-haired beauty seemed to be enjoying every minute of the journey. I remember being dumbstruck when she caught me looking at her, but pleased when she returned my gaze with a smile of amusement. I didn't think twice, and started walking toward her. I tried to be so polite…clicking both my heels together and making a slight bow when I asked her what part of Sweden she was from. To my surprise, she was so direct and straightforward with her answer, "Blekinge, and you?" There were no lowered eyes or shy giggles. My only thought was…this is not going to be easy!*

All I could say was, I am from Karlstad…the Varmlands.

Nils and Linnea 1910

She asked me where I was headed…I told her about my sister, Gerda, in North Cambridge and her husband, Gustav Frykberg. I even went on about my plans to find a job there as a woodworker.

I remember being so blindsided by talking to her that I forgot my interview!

Back at work on the floor of the factory, Nils had trouble

clearing his mind of the event and could only think of all the questions he had back then. *Were they traveling alone…with their parents or maybe an aunt or uncle? What were their plans when they arrived in Boston? Were they going to stay in the area or move on to Illinois or Minnesota like so many other Swedes? What was behind those mischievous blue eyes of the taller one who called herself Linnea?*

Taken with their conversation, Nils had forgotten the most important thing…his interview with the Head Purser. Excusing himself, he rushed to his bunk, pulled out his violin case, opened it and hoped that the precious envelope was still there! He was so relieved to find it tucked beneath the bow that he re-read the gold lettering on the front, just to be sure of the name…William E. Marshall, Head Purser, S.S. Saxonia. He turned the card over to check the time and read the hand-written note that explained that the bearer of this card, Nils Wansberg, had an appointment with Mr. Marshall on June 7, 1910 at 5:30 P.M. in the Head Purser's Office.

Nils's appointment was the result of the generous effort of his music teacher, Dr. Per Sorenson of Karlstad. Dr. Sorenson had lived in England for five years where he earned a doctorate of music degree from the London Institute of Music and Fine Arts. When he finished his studies, Dr. Sorenson returned to his hometown of Karlstad, where he hoped to establish a school of music with the financial backing of the wealthy businessmen in the area. Regrettably, the Swedish economy remained flat for a number of years and local businessmen never had the extra money to fund his idea, which at the time was considered a low community priority. In those lean years, Dr. Sorenson continued to support himself by providing private lessons to the locals, one of whom was young Nils Wansberg.

Nils's father, Emil, had introduced him to the violin at age twelve, but quickly realized the boy's talent was beyond his limited teaching abilities. When Nils turned fourteen, Emil brought him to Dr. Sorenson. Per was so impressed with the boy's natural talent that they worked out a bartering agreement to pay for violin lessons. Emil would bring a chicken, mutton, potatoes or whatever he could muster off his farm in exchange for Dr. Sorenson's time with Nils. Over the years, the lessons continued even though Emil was not always able to provide much in return. It really didn't matter to Dr. Sorenson, however, for he enjoyed teaching Nils, admiring both his work ethic and love of music. So when it came time for Nils to tell his long-time teacher that he was leaving Sweden for a new life in America, Per was deeply saddened, but at the same time, eager to provide Nils with whatever assistance he could.

When Per heard that Nils's itinerary included an Atlantic

crossing on the S.S. Saxonia, he immediately sent off a letter to Rodger Willowby, a London Institute classmate and London native who remained there after completing his studies. Per had maintained contact with Rodger, now a concert level cellist, who was currently playing first chair with the London Symphony. Dr. Sorenson remembered that a recent letter from Mr. Willowby mentioned his desire to take a break from the symphony routine to fill a position with a string quartet assigned to the Cunard Line. Per knew only too well, however, that this was just another of Rodger's many wild ideas that would never come to fruition. But that did not stop him from writing to Rodger for assistance in finding young Nils some work on the Cunard Line's, S.S. Saxonia. After an exchange of a few additional letters, Rodger had finally produced, through friends connected with Cunard, the small white envelope that Nils now held in his hand.

I remember feeling so rushed, thought Nils. *I had hoped that there was enough time to get dressed properly and hurried to unfold my suit, a white shirt, black bow tie and a pair of socks to get dressed. I remember that suit…it was all I had…a black four-button coat and matching black pants with a satin stripe down each side…the clothes I had used for recitals in Karlstad. I was panicked, standing in front of the mirror mounted above the dresser. I combed my hair straight back, brushed my moustache and tried to get a better look at the whole effect. I wished the mirror were a bit larger or lower so I might see how the length of the pants covered my shoes.*

Nils laughed out loud when he remembered how he jumped up in the air in the hope of catching a glimpse of his shoes. *It was only after the third jump that I realized I couldn't see my shoes and that I must have looked a bit silly. My roommates were giving me disapproving stares and when I realized that this was the best I could do, I picked up my violin, and walked out of the dormitory into the lounge through a door marked "Upper Levels".*

Nils climbed two flights of stairs only to find that at the top, there was a locked gate. Fortunately, before long, a young man dressed in white from head to toe, passed by the gate. The young man stopped and turned toward Nils with a quizzical look. He didn't know quite what to make of this man in a black suit who carried what seemed to be a violin case. Nils saw his confusion and blurted out in his broken English "I have a note please" as he quickly removed the envelope from his jacket and thrust it through the gate.

After some hesitation, the young man in white took the envelope from Nils and began to read the card inside. Apparently not convinced or not sure what to do, he finally held up his hand to Nils and said simply, "A moment please."

With that, he disappeared down the corridor.

Nils, at this point, had not been overly anxious and hoped the boy was going off to consult with some higher authority. Sure enough, the boy returned after a few minutes and now asked, "Papers please". Nils did not read or write English very well but understood a good deal thanks to Dr. Sorenson who would speak English during his violin lessons. What the young man had just said to him, however, did not register and given the look on his face, the boy tried another tact and said "Passport please". This Nils understood and dutifully passed his passport through the gate without giving it much thought. The boy took the document from Nils and once again disappeared down the corridor. Panic-stricken, Nils realized that he had just given up two of his three most valuable possessions to a fourteen-year old boy!

Finishing his lunch, Nils thought, *My God, I might as well have given him the violin too and be done with it. And he was fourteen! I had a dog at home older than that. What will I do if this man-child never returns? Not to mention that I was so desperate to go to the bathroom!*

Between the mental distraction of the meeting with Linnea and his haste to get ready for the interview, Nils completely forgot to take care of this necessity. Now he was in a real predicament. If he went back down to the lounge bathroom to relieve himself, he might miss the return of the boy.

Oh God where is that kid? Here I am all dressed up, my violin in hand and about to pee all over myself, he muttered under his breath. *A fine impression I'll make…that is if I ever get the chance. Where is he?*

It seemed like an eternity to Nils. When the young man finally returned, a gentleman who appeared to be of authority, wearing a gold stripe on his sleeve and an impressive looking white cap, accompanied him. The man in the cap unlocked the gate, slid it back far enough for Nils to pass through and said the magic words, "Mr. Wansberg …please follow me."

Once Nils passed through the gate two things happened. First, and much to his relief, the man with the stripe on his sleeve and a gold nametag that read Harold Robbins, returned his passport. Second, Nils had to quickly make the decision to ask for directions to the nearest bathroom, as he knew the Head Purser's office, no matter how close, would not be close enough for him to wait any longer. With that in mind he quickly took the passport from Mr. Robbins and said with a slight bow and a smile, "Would it be possible to use the bathroom please?"

Mr. Robbins gave him a disapproving look and, without saying a word, continued walking down the corridor for about twenty steps until finally stopping in front of a door with "Gentlemen" written in bold black letters.

Mr. Robbins gave the impression that it was beneath him to be escorting a passenger from the steerage quarters through "his" section of first class. His attitude toward Nils was one of condescending reluctance. His cold aloofness did not go unnoticed by young Nils but at this juncture he was more interested in the mundane service the bathroom could provide.

Now relieved, Nils was able to take notice of the surroundings he had failed to observe when he first rushed through the door. If a washroom were any indication of what first class accommodations were like, he couldn't wait to see the rest of the ship. The gleaming white porcelain washbowl was balanced on top of a tapered pedestal base fashioned from the same material. Four-lobe porcelain handles each centered with the gold letters "H" and "C" for hot and cold turned on gold-plated faucets. Directly above the washbowl hung a large mirror framed in ornately carved wood approximately three inches wide. The floor was made of an intricate pattern of black and white one-inch square ceramic tiles that gave the appearance of a large checkerboard. Nils could have spent another half hour looking at the walls, light fixtures, wood paneling, but he didn't want to keep Mr. Robbins waiting any longer than necessary. Even for the short time that he had been in the washroom, he was sure that Mr. Robbins was already impatiently pacing the outside corridor muttering to himself about having to babysit a Swedish immigrant. Nils quickly finished washing his hands, wiped them on the white towel with the red embroidered letters "S.S. SAXONIA", and pushed open the narrow wooden door.

Just as he thought, when he stepped out into the corridor, he found Mr. Robbins with his arms crossed and a distasteful look on his face. "Now can we please hurry Mr. Wansberg," he said sternly, while gazing at his pocket watch. "We only have but a few minutes if we are to reach the Head Purser's office on time."

Nils was not intimidated. With a quick smile, his head bowed, and a sweep of his arm, he pointed down the corridor and said in his best English, "After you kind sir."

Whenever Nils ran across a person like Mr. Robbins, he had difficulty comprehending what gave them that sense of superiority. It was an elitist view that he very rarely encountered in Sweden. With no malice, he just saw it as a peculiar personality trait.

Nils was one of twelve children and like most Swedish families he had grown up on a farm where everyone was expected to contribute. It didn't matter if you were older, taller, stronger or smarter. That only meant that you were expected to do more according to your particular strength. There was absolutely no room for thoughts of superiority or special treatment, as it would disrupt the overall performance of the farm and cause an unbalanced workload that would not be tolerated by the majority. It was sort of an unwritten checks and balance system that worked like a mini-democracy. You were expected to share by necessity the clothes, books and the few toys that were handed down from old to young. Through it all, Nils had developed a very laid back, calm and unassuming personality that viewed a person such as Mr. Robbins as a rather humorous oddity.

Walking at a brisk pace, Mr. Robbins hadn't given Nils much time to look at his surroundings. But Nils did take note of the wood-paneled narrow corridor and the floor, which was covered with a brightly colored red and green diamond patterned rug. He took in the stained wood panels and on the opposite wall, the brass portholes. Since it was summer, most of the portholes were open and a refreshing breeze blew through the corridor. Nils could see that the ocean was calm and was able to catch a glimpse of passengers in deck chairs with the sun at their backs.

While trying to keep up with Mr. Robbins, Nils wasn't able to take in as much of the sights as he would have liked, but he hoped there would be other opportunities if all went well with his interview. The chance to view more of the ship was not only for his own gratification but, more importantly, to build up a reservoir of information that he could relate to Linnea whom he hoped to see that evening. He couldn't wait to describe the events of the afternoon to her and found it difficult to concentrate on his upcoming interview.

They arrived at Mr. Marshall's office in plenty of time, despite the concerns of Mr. Robbins. Although Mr. Marshall had the appearance of a typical stuffy regimental English gentleman, he turned out to be a very warm, charming and considerate person. His jet-black hair, parted down the middle, slicked back close to his head was held neatly in place with whatever Vaseline concoction was popular at the time. His hair shone even though the room was dimly lit. He had mutton chop sideburns and, as if to keep perfect symmetry, his moustache was also parted in the middle and neatly waxed back to either side. He wore gold "Ben Franklin" style wire rimmed glasses with lenses that were only slightly larger than his eyes. They were balanced precariously at the end of his nose, obviously used for reading only. Nils was close to five feet eight, which was considered average, but when Mr. Marshall stood up from behind his desk to shake hands, he towered over Nils by a good seven inches. Unlike most of the ship's crew, William E. Marshall was dressed in a brown three-piece suit and spilling out from the top of his vest was a loop of a gold chain that Nils assumed must have been attached to a fashionable pocket watch appropriate for a man of his position.

After the perfunctory introductions, he made Nils feel most welcome by offering him a well-cushioned chair to sit in and insisting that he have a cup of tea along with a choice of biscuits and small cakes that were served on an elegant silver tray.

Mr. Marshall explained that when he first learned of Nils through mutual acquaintances, he thought that the ship's string quartet might be able to use him as an alternate or possibly an occasional soloist. But unfortunately, the members of the quartet were not very receptive to the idea. He went on to explain that he was ready to drop the matter, but when he casually mentioned Nils to the Captain at dinner, much to his surprise, the Captain began to talk about a plan he had been harboring for the past several months. His idea was that a violinist would serenade the patrons at the evening meal and possibly in the smoke room or lounge. He felt that it would be an attraction not found on most steam liners. It could be used as a marketing tool or feature that could be expanded to the rest of the Cunard fleet.

Mr. Marshall then began to outline the details of his plan

to Nils. First of all, he had arranged for Nils to audition with one of the members of the string quartet that afternoon. Providing that Nils's skill was acceptable, he would begin tomorrow evening in the dining hall. He went on to clarify that the ship's crew was busy making preparations for their arrival at Queenstown, Ireland next morning, and that it would not be possible for Nils to start this evening. He went on to outline the details of this new plan. The agreement was for Nils to play every evening from 6:00 until 10:00 P.M. He was to begin the following night and play each night until they arrived in Boston. He was to be paid ten U.S. dollars for his services, which he would receive upon docking in Boston.

Mr. Marshall made it clear to Nils that the Captain was adamant that, under no circumstances, was he to accept tips from the patrons. The Captain had thought it highly inappropriate for first class passengers, who had paid one hundred and fifty dollars for the trip, to feel obligated to pay for the music. In fact, he insisted that Mr. Marshall provide cards at each table that would explain this and urged Mr. Marshall to alert all the waiters that this was a new and free service offered only by the Cunard Line. Additionally, he announced that Mr. Robbins should meet Nils at the gate each evening at 5:00 P.M. to escort him to the dining hall.

The interview ended with Mr. Marshall handing Nils

five of his business cards to be used in case Mr. Robbins was needed elsewhere and unable to meet him at the gate on any particular night. Whoever was sent to take Mr. Robbins place would require some form of identification to allow Nils to pass through. He gave Nils a firm and vigorous handshake, wished him the best of luck on his audition, and told him not to hesitate to visit if there should be any questions or problems with the arrangement as outlined in their meeting.

The audition was something of a non-event, lasting no more than thirty minutes. A reluctant Mr. Robbins had escorted Nils to a small office located only a short walk away from the Head Purser. Awaiting him was one, Howard Wallace, who played violin in the ship's string quartet. Mr. Wallace, although polite, could not hide his annoyance at having to conduct an audition due to what he considered a rather ill conceived idea of the Captain. *How embarrassing* he thought, *to have some Swedish farmer, playing God knows what, in such an elegant setting as the first class dining hall.* In any event, he was not one to shirk his responsibility and, without much fanfare, quickly instructed Nils to play the music of his choosing whenever he was ready.

Nils was not the least bit nervous, being well prepared from the countless recitals arranged for him over the years by his good friend and mentor Dr. Sorenson. He calmly removed his violin and bow from its case and, without any warm-up, began to play a popular Vienna Waltz that he thought might be appropriate.

The door was open to the small room where Nils was auditioning and after a few minutes it seemed that anyone and everyone within earshot was now peering in to see from where these beautiful sounds were coming. It wasn't long before the crowd outside the door had grown to more than fifteen people—all of whom were perfectly silent and mesmerized by the music. When Nils finished his piece, there was a momentary pause and then, as if someone had snapped their finger to awake them out of a hypnotic state, the small crowd began to clap in approval. Nils, maintaining his usual quiet confidence, and without hesitation, responded with an appreciative smile, followed by a slight bow.

Mr. Wallace immediately stood up from his wicker chair to disperse the small but rather enthusiastic group. "The show is over everyone", he confirmed, nervously clearing his throat. "Now will you please excuse us as Mr. Wansberg and I have some private business to discuss."

Minutes before, while Nils was playing, Mr. Wallace was mulling over what he would say to Nils at the end of the audition. Prior to hearing Nils play, he had a firm plan to give an early burial to the Captain's idea. He would simply stop

Nils halfway through his rendition and tell him his performance was not acceptable. The mandatory apology would be given, he would tell the Head Purser of his decision and a merciful end to the project would certainly follow. No one would be the wiser and certainly this immigrant from Sweden would not offer any resistance to the decision.

But now everything had changed. His prejudice toward the Captain's brainstorm was completely diminished by the superb skill of young Nils. Mr. Wallace was a professional and as such recognized when a musician was able to transfer his passion for music to an audience. It was that extra ingredient that always separated the truly talented from the ordinary. Even if he wanted to deny Nils his chance, it would have been impossible. The audition was not far from the Head Purser's office, and with the door wide open, Mr. Marshall surely had either heard the music first hand or would soon hear about it from one of the onlookers.

When Mr. Wallace closed the door, he faced Nils and said, "In all honesty, Mr. Wansberg, I have to admit that I made a rather large mistake in pre-judging your abilities. My strong opposition to the Captain's idea seems to have prejudiced my thoughts toward the musician that was to carry out the concept. In point of fact, I may very well be guilty of attempting to kill both the message and the messenger. Your audition, however, has jolted me back to reality. It is obvious, even to the untrained ear, that you possess the skills of an accomplished violinist. So the short of it is, Mr. Wansberg, that I am prepared to tell Mr. Marshall that we should feel very fortunate to have you on board". Somewhat tongue in cheek he continued, "Although, at the same time, I'm delighted that you will be disembarking in Boston as I fear for my position in the string quartet if you were to stay for the return trip."

Having finished with his short speech, they shook hands and Mr. Wallace opened the door where they found Mr. Robbins waiting in the corridor with a supercilious little smile on his face. Nils was not certain, but he suspected that Mr. Robbins had assumed, noticing the door was closed, that perhaps things had not gone so well with the audition. He probably expected Mr. Wallace to tell him to escort Mr. Wansberg back to the steerage section and that it would not be necessary to meet him at the gate tomorrow evening.

True to his expectations Mr. Wallace turned to him and announced, "Well hello Mr. Robbins, your timing is impeccable. Mr. Wansberg and I have just concluded our business. Would you be so kind and escort him back to his quarters please?" And, with that, Mr. Wallace began to close the door to the small audition room.

That was it, Mr. Robbins thought...*this folly has finally come to an end. After all, there was no mention that Nils had won the position.* He continued to play out the scenario in his head. *I'll walk the immigrant Swede back to the steerage section where he belongs, never to bother with him again. At long last my routine will return to normal.*

Just as he was beginning to become comfortable with the idea, Mr. Wallace opened the door and, almost as an afterthought said, "I'm certain you haven't forgotten, but it's important that you meet Mr. Wansberg, per Mr. Marshall's instructions, at the gate tomorrow by 5:00 P.M." He added, "We certainly would not want to deprive our dinner guests of the ship's new feature attraction". And then he gave one final instruction. "The maître di' will be informed of Mr. Wansberg's new role, so once you guide him to the dining hall the maitre di' will take care of the remaining details."

Nils glanced at Mr. Robbins only momentarily, but it was long enough to see his disdainful smile while most of the color disappeared from his face. The ashen Mr. Robbins could only muster a dutiful, "Of course sir."

The walk back to the steerage section was accomplished without a single word exchanged between the two men. The silence, however, was a welcome interlude for Nils; a perfect time to reflect on what had been one of the most eventful evenings of his life.

One of his first thoughts had been of his family. With eleven brothers and sisters there was never a shortage of willing listeners. Somehow, it had never seemed to matter whether the story or event was one of great joy or sadness as long as there was someone with whom to share. The happiness of recounting the event had increased in intensity proportional to the number of people willing to hear your story. Conversely, if the story was one of disappointment, the feeling of sadness was given a chance to dissipate among the willing participants. It had been a winning proposition no matter what the circumstance, and gave each member of the family a wonderful therapeutic outlet. *After all,* he thought, *what good was a story or an important event if there was no one around to tell it to?*

With that in mind, his thoughts turned to Linnea back in steerage. *How much fun it would be to describe all of what he had seen and done this evening,* he thought…*I wouldn't know where to begin.*

When Mr. Robbins and Nils arrived back at the gate that divided the first and second-class sections of the ship from steerage, it seemed to Nils that it was only moments before that he had been on the other side of this same gate anxiously waiting for someone to come by and let him through.

Mr. Robbins unlocked the gate and slid it back just enough for Nils to pass through. Always the gentleman, Nils turned to Mr. Robbins and said, "I am very grateful for all the help you have given me this afternoon." He declined to extend his hand, mostly in an effort not to obligate Mr. Robbins and partly for fear of having his gesture rejected. He accepted instead a brief condescending nod of acknowledgement from Mr. Robbins, and with that, Nils slipped through the gate.

Nils knew it must be late and hoped he could reach the lounge in time before Linnea and her sister retired for the evening. He flew down the one flight of steps using the railing as a brace to lift his body in the air so that he might skip three or more steps at a time.

It wasn't long before he reached his bunk where he quickly stooped down to stow his violin. He then rushed into the lounge and, as luck would have it, everyone was still up and about, which meant there was a good chance he would find Linnea. The lounge was crowded and those that could not find a seat on the long wooden benches were standing, making it difficult to navigate through the packed assembly. Almost everyone was engaged in loud conversation. The few lucky enough to find a writing table had paper in front of them and were trying desperately to concentrate on composing a letter to family and friends.

As Nils continued his search, he began to pick up several conversations in his native tongue. When he walked by these groups he would give a quick smile and say hello or good evening in Swedish. Rather than ask him to join in the conversation, however, all of them, to a person would give him this curious puzzled look, return his greeting and then promptly continue with their discussion. After the second or third encounter of this type he was really starting to become self-conscious. Just as he was beginning to run through a list of what might be causing this odd reaction, he finally spotted Linnea sitting on one of the benches in an animated conversation with a woman at least twice her age. Curiously, her sister was nowhere in sight.

Nils slowly approached and offered the best he could come up with, "Hello ladies." Now that he had their attention, he continued, "I don't mean to interrupt your conversation but I wanted to offer my apologies to Linnea for having left so abruptly earlier."

"Your name is Nils isn't it?" responded Linnea.

"Good memory", Nils answered.

Smiling with a slight smirk on her face, Linnea asked, "Is there a special event planned this evening?"

"Not that I know of", answered Nils. "Why do you ask?"

"Just wondering because it looks like you are dressed for

one," said Linnea with a smile.

Oh my God, Nils thought. *How stupid of me! In my haste I forgot to change clothes. I've still got on my black suit, white shirt and bow tie! No wonder everyone was avoiding me. They must have thought I was half-crazy, dressed this way in steerage class!*

He could feel his ears burning and there was nothing he could do to prevent his face from turning red.

"You know," he tried to explain; "I was so excited about what happened this evening with my audition and interview, that I completely forgot to change clothes. No wonder everyone was looking at me as if I had the plague."

Linnea made an attempt to take him seriously but failed miserably as she burst out in laughter. "I'm sorry," she said laughing, "but you look so ridiculously out of place. Handsome…but still very silly…the people in here were worried to death that you were about ready to check their passports and papers!"

Her laugh was somehow both disarming and infectious and Nils couldn't help but join her in the merriment, even though it was at his own expense. Her eyebrows lifted slightly, and with her eyes half-closed, she made no lady-like attempt to tone down the volume. The laugh was genuine as could be.

It had been a long while since Nils had a reason to laugh and it felt so good. "Oh my", he said as they both began to recover, "I can't remember the last time I had such a good laugh. Linnea, why don't you give me a moment to change and I'll meet you back here in fifteen minutes? We can have a nice long talk about my adventures today."

"Why that would be wonderful," Linnea said, "it will give me a chance to check in on my sister Frida. She's not feeling too well."

"See you shortly then", Nils said, as he pivoted, and walked away in the direction of the men's dormitory.

During the short walk back to the dormitory, Nils reflected on how refreshing and very different Linnea was from most Swedish women. He wondered where and how she developed such an open and spirited personality in a country known to produce women that were for the most part quiet, reserved and often times very shy. He could not even begin to presume the answer to that question just yet, but he certainly was determined to find out.

Several steps before he reached his bunk, Nils was already beginning to remove his bow tie and unbutton his shirt. Everything came off in a hurry and was thrown hastily on his bunk bed. He reached down below to retrieve his suitcase, unbuckled the two leather straps and opened it while it was still on the floor. He selected a plain grey shirt and a pair of brown corduroy pants and then literally threw his entire recital ensemble back into his suitcase. There was no time for folding or smoothing. The man was on a mission!

Nils was indeed in a hurry but not going to make any mistakes about his attire this time. He looked at himself in the dresser mirror checking to make sure buttons were secure, zippers zipped and collars straight. A quick brush to his hair and he was on his way back to the lounge.

Surprisingly, Linnea had already returned to the spot where he had left her, and as he approached she remarked, "Well now, you look much more comfortable." She motioned to the bench, "Let's have a seat and you can tell me all about your day. I am anxious to hear something exciting. My day in the dormitory has been so uninteresting."

They talked for hours, as Nils walked her through every detail about Mr. Robbins, Mr. Marshall, the audition and the elegant furnishings, even describing details of the first class bathroom. Her infectious laugh returned when he told the story about giving up his passport and waiting anxiously for someone to return while he stood behind the gate with his bladder ready to burst. Nils had not known her for long, but he already felt comfortable divulging this embarrassing detail.

Reluctantly, he mentioned that they were going to arrive

at Queenstown early next morning and that, perhaps, they
should both retire for the night.

FOUR

A Bit of a Breeze

The next morning, Linnea had awakened to thoughts of Nils. *I could have stayed up all night talking with him. He was so straightforward and I loved that he could laugh at himself. Too bad Frida was still upset that I was up half the night talking to someone I didn't even know. After all we were on a boat...what could happen?*

The sun was just rising when she sat up, and thought of the next big event. *The boat is stopping at Queenstown to pick up passengers this morning...I can't wait to practice my English on the Irish that will be boarding!*

She dressed in a hurry and went to the first window she could find. She saw land but the ship had stopped just short of the harbor. At first she was puzzled, but then remembered what she had read when planning their journey...the Cunard

Line had special jetties where passengers boarded tenders that took them out to the ships moored near the harbor entrance! When the tender pulled alongside the Saxonia, Linnea saw huge crowds—friends and family that were seeing their relatives off to America. She remembered that they called it an "Irish Wake" when someone left Ireland…they usually never returned. She was so caught up in the excitement that she didn't see Nils approaching. He was hoping to talk to her again but couldn't find a way to get her attention amidst all of this commotion. Luggage, trunks and cargo were thrown down and people milled about getting into each other's way. Linnea could feel the excitement of the people boarding as they called out to one another in a language she couldn't quite understand. Bells clanged and steam hissed through the boilerplate and soon they were enveloped in the mist of the damp early morning air. Suddenly, a young woman with a small trunk in tow swung around and bumped into Linnea.

"Oh, sorry, I didn't see ya…I beg your pardon Miss," said the young woman. "I don't know where I am going…so much commotion…can you tell me where we put our tings?"

Linnea smiled…she was happy to help her and was eager to find out what these Irish people were like. "What's your name?" she asked her. "And you don't have to call me miss. My name is Linnea."

The young woman was about twenty-two, the same age as Linnea, She had dark curly hair that seemed determined to escape from under the hat that she wore. Laughing she replied, "Bridey's the name, pleased to meet you. You're dressed so nicely that all I could tink of was to call you Miss. Could ya help me, if ya have the time?"

She talked so quickly that Linnea had trouble understanding her. "Come this way," Linnea said as she took her hand, "I'll help you with your trunk." Together they descended down the stairs to the third class quarters. Nils, who had been watching from a distance, decided he would have to wait to find Linnea alone again. He hoped that she didn't think he was a fool after last night.

Once they were in the dormitory, Linnea showed Bridey where she could put her clothes. The drawers were filling up quickly. The Irish contingent was in full force, banging their cases around and quickly claiming their space while loudly chattering at high speed. Linnea was amazed at how relaxed these young women were in their new surroundings. In one corner of the room, two women were going at it, fighting over drawer space.

"Piss off, I was here first," the older woman said.

"You'd be talkin like you'd been aboard for days…I believe we both got here at the same time!" the younger woman

54

fired back.

Linnea loved listening to them…she had never heard such back and forth. She was so used to the Nordic reserve of her people. This was going to be a good trip…she was more excited than ever about this new journey.

Meanwhile, Nils had gone back to his quarters only to find chaos. The Irish men had arrived and were joking around as if they had known each other for years. Confused, Nils thought to himself, *how could they all have known each other…were they all from the same place?*

A young man stood by his bunk and had flung his case on the upper bed. With a great smile he stuck out his hand and said, "Jack Farrissey here." Nils put out his hand and the man grabbed it with such force that he wondered if he would ever play the violin again. Then Farissey slapped him on the back, pulled Nils toward him, looked him in the eye and said, "Looks like we're mates for a while."

Nils was taken aback and thought…*this is going to be a long trip.* He felt awkward watching this Farrissey person unpack his things but it didn't take long—he didn't have much in the way of clothes. Then Farrissey clapped his hands, reached into his coat and took out what looked like a tin whistle. *Now,* thought Nils, *I'm interested.*

Slowly, Farrissey started to play his tin whistle. It was an eerie, sad and wistful tune. He had only played a few bars before another young man had taken out his fiddle and began to join him in this song that seemed a plaintive goodbye to the land that they had just left…a song of mourning. Nils was amazed at how quickly the other men joined in and were putting words to the music…he listened and sat fascinated by what they were singing.

"I wish I was in Carrickfergus
Only for nights in Ballygrand,
I would swim over the deepest ocean,
Only for nights in Ballygrand.
But the sea is wide and I cannot cross over,
And neither have I the wings to fly,
I wish I could meet a handsome boatman,
To ferry me over to my love and die.

But in Kilkenny, it is reported,
They have marble stones there, as black as ink,
With gold and silver I would support her,
But I'll sing no more now 'till I have a drink,
For I'm drunk today, and I'm seldom sober,
A handsome rover from town to town,
Ah, but I'm sick now, my days are numbered,
Come all you young men and lay me down."

The music was so moving that Nils felt sad. Never had music had such an effect on him. He realized that even though he was eager for a new life, he would miss his family and Karlstad…and he hadn't allowed himself those feelings. The chorus of "lay me down" was repeated over and over and then, much to Nil's surprise, the tempo picked up and there was another kind of tune that was very different. Before he knew it, Nils was tapping his toes to music that he had never heard before. He had never experienced such a range of emotion. He was bewildered by his feelings. *How could these people play music that would take you to so many places?*

Suddenly, the music stopped and the man called Farrissey, raised his hand and said,

"Let's go to the lounge for a good craic! It's too crowded in here. We need to move around…dance, have a houli."

With that, they took off for the lounge. Nils was tempted to follow them but realized he had to get ready for this evening's performance.

Meanwhile, Linnea was trying to help her sister with her seasickness as the ship was going through a rough patch of high seas. Frida was miserable. Linnea could only think of going up to the lounge to see what was going on there. She was dying to find out what they all were going to do once they arrived. It would help her in her search for a job that she needed to make the fare to Piper City. When she saw that Frida was finally asleep in spite of the din of the Irish girls' chatter, she decided to wander over to the other side of the room where Bridie was sitting on the edge of her bed talking to one of the other Irish girls about where she was going when she arrived in Boston.

Linnea decided to join their conversation and asked Bridie, "Do you know what you are going to do when we arrive?"

"Oh yea," Bridie replied, "my sister Maureen, who works in Cambridge, fixed something up with a family there; I'm to work doing their laundry. My sister works in the kitchen in the same house. Do you have a job yet?"

"No I haven't thought of it" Linnea said, "I don't know anybody in Boston…only my brother Victor in Piper City, Illinois. But I'll need to make some money to take the train there. I'm also travelling with my sister."

"Well, maybe Maureen can fix you up…she knows lots of people. Would you be liking a tummytoe?" Bridie asked in her Cork accent. "I pinched them at the greengrocers just be- fore we left."

Linnea had no idea what a tummytoe was but said, "Yes, thanks.

Bridie reached into her basket, and produced a beautiful

tomato. Linnea laughed when she finally figured out what Bridie was offering. It had been several days since she had eaten anything fresh…so far, the meals in steerage had been awful…watery soup, stale bread and some boiled beef—not exactly a smorgasbord.

"Tell me, what is Boston like? Does your sister Maureen tell you about life there in her letters? Is it hard to get a job there?" asked Linnea. But soon she felt that she was asking too many questions and slowed down.

Bridie looked her over and said, "Well from what I've seen of you, you're a Protestant; I haven't heard much rattling of the beads from your direction and I don't suppose Sweden has many Catholics. No offense, but it's a good thing for you. Maureen tells me that "Protestant" is often listed as a necessary job qualification. From what she says we Irish are big in politics but most of us are still going to have to work with our hands to get food on the table. I heard that even businessmen who needed a loan couldn't get one if they're Catholic. Still most Irish have a good craic in a town like Boston…there's so many of us there. Speaking of a good craic, let's go up on the deck. Maybe there's something going on."

Linnea was grateful for this new friendship, settling into an ambitious routine of dividing her time between Bridie, Nils and Frida. She would meet with Nils every morning after breakfast and they would talk about what it was like performing in the dining hall. She was fascinated by his descriptions of the first class passengers; how they dressed, how they talked, the food they ate, even the jewelry they wore. Nils, who at times would also play in the lounge or the smoking room, would describe those scenes to her in infinite detail. He also had made fast friends with the Italian chef, who admired his music and always managed to invite Nils into the kitchen for a plate of food during his breaks. Each night, after Nils had finished with his playing, the chef would wrap a pastry in a napkin and stuff it into his suit pocket. Nils would never eat it but saved it for Linnea as part of the ritual of their morning talk.

Linnea's afternoons were spent with Bridie, who never seemed short of things to say or do. She could not get over her energy and bold talk. The old standard inquiry about wondering what's underneath the surface of an individual did not apply to Bridie. You could always tell what she was feeling. Even though Linnea had similar personality traits, she had never been able to fully express herself in such a reserved society as Sweden. For her, it was both exhilarating and liberating to see a woman such as Bridie speaking her mind without much regard to the consequences. They became fast friends talking freely about everything under the sun: men, cooking, babies, work, America, family and everything in between.

The balance of her time was used up with her sister Frida who was not very seaworthy. Unfortunately, she spent most of the day in bed with a basin nearby. Linnea felt sorry for Frida, but at the same time relieved that she was temporarily confined to her bed and unable to prevent her from talking with Nils or Bridie as often as she liked. Even as sick as Frida was, she would constantly admonish Linnea for talking to Nils or associating with that "tramp of a woman" Bridie. Whatever strength she had, it was completely spent on berating Linnea for her supposed sins.

Nils, on the other hand, was fast becoming friends with Jack Farrissey. After Nils returned from work, they sometimes would sit on deck and talk. Jack came from a fishing village on the southern coast of Ireland and one night he told Nils how his brother built his first boat.

"You know, my brother never built a boat before, but he had seen one he liked down in the boat cove. He didn't have much schooling so he got some plain paper from the butcher and brought it down to the cove and traced the shape of the boat's stern. Then he built himself a band saw, got some wood and started to build what turned out a few months later to be a beautiful boat. From then on he was hooked!" Jack laughed and slapped his knee. "But here's the best part…the next boat he wanted to build was real big one—a twenty-five footer. But the ting was, the shed he had out back was not high enough, and he knew some of the neighbors would get the guards on the case if he raised the roof. So you know what he did?" Nils couldn't imagine and shook his head in a no.

"Well, he dug down into the ground a couple of feet—that's how he was able to fit in the new boat. I tell you that boat was a real beauty by the time he finished it—inboard engine and all!"

Nils was amazed at how clever Jack's brother must have been. He loved hearing stories like this. *I can't wait to get to work again*, Nils thought to himself, as he stretched out his hands. "You know", he said, "I am hoping to get work in a framer's shop in Boston. I have heard that there is a Swedish woodcarver there that is making frames for museums and many fine painters of the day. People in Karlstad told me that artists and their patrons don't want mass-produced frames and are looking for fine craftsmanship."

It was close to midnight before they both agreed that it was getting late and they should head back to the dormitory for a good night's rest. Nils was not one to dwell on the past, but the energy and excitement of the day was still with him and he was unable to sleep. Instead he allowed himself to drift back and take account of the circumstances that had brought him to this stage of his life. The discussion he had earlier with Jack about finding work as a framer evoked a tinge of anxiety as he wondered how difficult it was really going to be. He was well trained in carpentry, but letters from his sister indicated stiff competition in Boston for jobs at that level.

FIVE

Time to Leave

At age fifteen in 1901, Nils's father, Emil, had suggested it was time he learned a trade other than agriculture. It was becoming increasingly difficult to make a living from farming and, with twelve children to support, Emil knew it would be best for many of them to find training in non-agrarian occupations. Moreover, his current status in the military was extremely precarious due to an impending change in Sweden's system of recruitment that was scheduled to take place that year. It meant that he might not be able to hold on to the farm for much longer and would have to move the family into the city of Karlstad.

From 1620 to 1901 Sweden had adopted an allotment system that cleverly put the burden of supporting an army directly on the citizens. Each province was to provide for a regiment of soldiers that consisted of twelve hundred men. Accordingly, each province was divided into twelve hundred districts called "rotes". The farmers from each rote were responsible for providing one soldier who would participate in a couple of brief training periods during the year. If war were to break out, he would be available immediately for quick mobilization.

The manner in which the farmers of a rote would support a soldier was to give him a parcel of land on which there was a small cottage or "croft" with a barn. Additionally, the farmers were to supply the soldier with enough grain and hay to support the soldier's parcel of land. It was an arrangement the farmers were willing to bear in exchange for an exempt status from military service.

In 1884 at the age of twenty, Emil Nilsson was chosen by the farmers of his rote to be the soldier for their district. It was something of an honor at the time, giving a young man such as Emil some social status in the community. A contract was drawn up and later ratified by the Captain of the regiment. Included in the contract was an additional and distinctive last name given to the new recruit by the farmers of the rote. This practice was one of wartime practicality peculiar to the Swedes. There were so many Nilssons, Anderssons, Olssons, etc. that one could imagine the problem of a lieutenant calling out, "Andersson, cover our left flank!" He would probably have twenty of his men, all Anderssons, stand up in unison responding to his command. As a result, Emil Nilsson became Emil Nilsson Wansberg; the Wansberg surname assigned to him by the farmers and later confirmed by the Captain of his regiment.

Sweden was at peace during the time Emil was in the army and, outside of a few brief periods of training during the year, Nils enjoyed the presence of his father on their farm. While the croft was small and crowded, the loft in the barn served as an extension of their living quarters with beds for the older children. He often thought of staying up until midnight in the loft with his older brothers and sisters while waiting for the New Year of 1900 to arrive. It was exciting to hear all of the church bells in the province ring as they announced the beginning of a new century. Plus, with all of the many farm animals and open space, it was an ideal place for the exploration and play of a young boy. Even though life in this environment could be difficult, especially during the harsh winters with some food shortages, Nils would never forget the promise of outdoor dinner gatherings during the long summer evenings when the sun seemingly refused to set. Between daily chores, school and his violin lessons, it was a childhood that nourished his curiosity.

In 1901, however, the military allotment system, which allowed Nils and his family to enjoy the country style of living, changed to a government-financed mandatory conscription program. This meant the farmers no longer would have to support a soldier. The rote would be dissolved and the croft, barn and land would all be returned to them. Emil, who had by now risen to the rank of a non-commissioned officer, would be forced to move his family to the city of Karlstad where his infantry would be in a government barracks. There, he would receive a small salary paid by the Crown or an even smaller pension if he chose to retire.

It was under these circumstances that Nils began an apprenticeship under a master craftsman named Gunnar Johnsrud. Nils's violin teacher, Per Sorenson, had very strong connections within the city of Karlstad and had recommended Gunnar. Mr. Johnsrud specialized in cabinet making. He was recognized as the best in Karlstad and commanded several prestigious clients including the city's mayor. Dr. Sorenson knew that Nils, because of his creative talents, would be better working with wood than some of the other apprentices in the foundries where brute strength was required.

Until 1846, the practice of learning a trade involved a series of well-defined steps. A young boy would start out as an apprentice in order to learn the basics of the trade under the tutelage of a master craftsman. The next rung up the ladder was a journeyman, whereby an apprentice would earn this title by creating a qualifying piece of work or "gesallprov". The journeyman then, true to his name, would in effect journey around the province gaining experience under different masters until he himself qualified as a master craftsman by taking an exam approved by the guild.

The system was more lenient at the time Nils entered as an apprentice, but Gunnar Johnsrud was a strict and demanding teacher who maintained the discipline of the old rules. Nils thrived under his tutelage and quickly learned the finer points of cabinet making. Even though it was no longer required, Gunnar insisted that Nils produce a "qualifying work" in order to consider him as a journeyman. It took Nils several months to complete, but he was finally rewarded for his efforts with the official title of journeyman. Gunnar duly approved his qualifying work. That most important "gesallprov" now lay stowed safely beneath his bunk on the SS Saxonia…it was his violin.

As he thought about his two mentors, Per Sorensen and Gunnar Johnsrud, Nils realized that he had mastered two skills that would somehow allow him to survive whatever challenges awaited him in America. Satisfied, he drifted off into a deep sleep.

After his last evening performance, Nils received the ten dollars, as promised, from the Head Purser, Mr. Marshall. In addition, and much to his surprise, he was also given a letter signed by the Captain which stated his appreciation for Nils's successful efforts in bringing the concept of a serenading musician into reality. He went on to comment about the numerous compliments he had received from the first class passengers and that Nils was in large part responsible for establishing the serenading musician as a permanent fixture aboard the Saxonia. The Captain closed the short letter by extending his best wishes and giving a strong recommendation of Nils's talent for any organization wishing to employ him.

Nils said his farewells to the members of the string quartet, the staff of the dining hall and finally to the Italian chef, who—after giving Nils an unexpected and embarrassing kiss on both cheeks—placed an extra pastry in his suit pocket.

Now all that remained was his final escort back to the steerage section by Mr. Robbins. Although their relationship had been strained at the beginning, albeit through no fault of Nils, the crusty British exterior of Mr. Robbins began to wear away ever so slowly during each successive walk back to the steel gate that separated their two worlds. For Nils, it was a most welcome and gratifying experience to see Mr. Robbins reveal the very human and sometimes soft underbelly of his personality. Over time, he had begun to realize that Nils was not only well respected for his musical talents but also genuinely appreciated by the entire staff for his sociability, calm demeanor and most of all his keen sense of humor. It seemed pointless to him to ignore Nils's attempts at conversation. At long last, Mr. Robbins began to unravel, ever so slowly and sometimes painfully, as he started to talk about his family, England and his profession.

When they arrived back at the gate for the final time, Nils reached into his vest pocket, pulled out a silver dollar and offered it to Mr. Robbins. Nils had accumulated four of these silver dollars courtesy of a "Big" Bob Connors from the great state of Texas, as he would boisterously introduce himself. Two things were certain when Big Bob appeared in the ship's dining hall; number one he would always be uproariously drunk, and second he would be sure to liberally distribute a pocket-full of silver dollars to the dining hall staff for favors as minor as a water refill.

Harold immediately backed away a half step, looking at the silver dollar as if it were a poisonous serpent. "Oh my, Mr Wansberg, this is highly irregular, that is to say it's against the ship's regulations, I…I can't possibly accept this," Harold stammered.

"I don't think you understand", Nils countered. "I really don't want you to keep it, but rather I wish for you to give it away." And with that statement Harold was now completely bewildered and the expression on his face let Nils know that an explanation was required.

"You see Harold", Nils continued, "coming from a large family and living in a country of poor farmers I learned early on that sharing and compassion for one another was sometimes a method of survival. The few times our small farm did better than average my father would always share some of the bounty with neighbors who had not been so fortunate. He always said it made him feel better, plus he knew the favor would be returned if the situation was reversed."

Harold's expression started to relax as he began to comprehend where Nils was going.

"So I hope that during one of your trips from Liverpool to America you will befriend someone much like myself, a poor immigrant from the steerage section, and give this silver dollar to them. I guarantee it will help you as much as it will them."

Seemingly satisfied with the explanation, Harold then accepted the silver dollar and a farewell handshake from Nils.

"Mr. Wansberg"…he hesitated…"I mean Nils…the very best of luck to you sir!"

Nils looked at him with a smile and said, "Well, Harold, that's the very first time you've called me by my first name. There's hope for you yet!" And with that, Nils slipped through the partially opened gate and began to walk down the steps leading towards the steerage section. He paused for a moment as he heard the click of the gate locking behind him for the very last time.

Nils could not allow himself to think any more about his adventure on the Saxonia but focused on what was at hand. *Tomorrow will be a big day, meeting up with Linnea, Frida and Bridie to navigate through the customs process...and getting settled with my sister and brother-in-law, Gustav.*

SIX

The Wind at their Back

The ship's horn blasted as it pulled into Cunard's wharf in East Boston. *The days had gone quickly,* Nils thought. *I've seen Linnea most mornings and those evenings when we had a chance to talk into the night after I finished playing were wonderful. I don't want it to end. I'm glad we decided to meet again after we get settled. I hope she's able to hold onto Gerda's address...but who knows where that small slip of paper will end up?*

All four of them went through immigration easily and now they were pushing through the crowd. Linnea and Frida held onto one another and tried to follow Bridie who seemed hell-bent on getting out of there. Linnea looked around for Nils but had lost sight of him. She panicked. All she had was that slip of paper. Linnea was confused by the size of this city.

It was larger than anything she had ever seen. There was chaos on the dock with most people shoving and anxiously looking for someone they knew. Bridie, who had Linnea and Frida in tow, was making her way toward a woman on the wharf who was waving frantically. "Maureen, Maureen" Bridie shouted as she pushed through the crowd toward her sister.

Quite a number of Bridie's relatives had come to greet her. They had so many questions about family that they had left behind in Ireland. They talked so fast that Linnea couldn't keep up and she stayed close to Bridie—she didn't want to lose her. Frida, who was feeling much better now that she was on land, looked around warily. They headed off to the East Boston Ferry, which would take them to Boston where they could catch a streetcar. On the ferry, Linnea looked back at the dock, which was getting smaller, still wondering where Nils was.

In a short time, they reached the other side of the bay and were on land again. Boarding the streetcar, Maureen who was so excited to see her sister safe and sound, wiped a tear, and proclaimed: "Now we're off." Linnea was overwhelmed and she thought that if it hadn't been for Bridie, she would have felt totally lost. Bridie realized that she hadn't heard a word from the two sisters. She reassured them that they were headed for Somerville, a town three miles north of Boston and that they'd sort things out when they got there.

In 1910, Boston was America's fifth-largest city. It was a city teeming with immigrants, most of them Irish. As they rode the trolley through Boston, Linnea noticed a man in a large touring car waving to people on the street. She asked Maureen who it was and she said, "Oh that's John F. Fitzgerald, "Honey Fitz" as we call him, he's running for mayor. Too bad we are not on the street or he would stop and give us his usual blarney…it goes like this…if my car were as big as my heart, I'd give you all a ride! You know he's the champion for the rights of the working Irish. I love that man!"

Linnea thought that it must be nice for the Irish to have a hero, someone to fight for their rights. She wondered if the Swedes had anyone like that to represent them. Linnea would have been hard pressed to find a Swedish politician in Boston at the time, even though there were over a million first and second-generation Swedish immigrants living in the U.S. Many didn't stop in Boston but went on to heavily wooded states like Minnesota and Wisconsin where the land was very much like Sweden. Those that settled in urban areas figured that the labor markets of the big cities would have more to offer cash-starved immigrants than the farm regions.

Life wasn't easy in the city for immigrants. New arrivals were three times more likely than natives to be on welfare in

1909 and a third were illiterate. But the Swedes were literate—by the late 18th century literacy in Sweden was already ninety percent.

At the time that Nils and Linnea arrived in Boston, the impact of immigration had contributed to low wages and poor working conditions. The majority of Scandinavians living in Boston had found work in the skilled trades. Nils was confident that as a craftsman, he had a much better chance of finding work than unskilled workers. Gerda, in her letters, had reassured him that he would find work.

On the trolley that was taking them to Somerville, Linnea saw street after street lined with double and triple-decker houses. *They are so large, yet close together,* she thought. *Nothing at all like the simple cottages in Ronneby.* She had no idea that she had arrived in what was the most densely populated city in New England.

The conductor shouted out, "Porter Square next stop!" Maureen pulled on Linnea's sleeve, announcing that they all should get off at the next stop.

They scrambled off the trolley with their luggage and baskets and started to walk the six blocks to Harvard Place. Meanwhile, the temperature had been steadily climbing since they had taken the ferry. It was the first time Linnea had been in such hot weather and she wished that she hadn't worn her wool dress. She had noticed that women on the streetcar were wearing cotton shirtwaists and lightweight skirts. She felt out of place…and unbearably hot!

They trudged up a hill and turned into a small lane where Maureen lived. "Well, we're here," Maureen said, pointing to the very large house at the end of the lane. Inside, young women were scurrying around setting the table for dinner. Linnea could hear pots and pans being banged around in the kitchen and the girls laughing as they talked back and forth while they cooked the meal. Upstairs, there was a long hall with rooms on either side. Maureen stopped at one of the rooms and said, "You can leave your things in here and we'll find a mattress for you three."

They put down their bags and Linnea and Frida looked at each other. They both were thinking the same thing…*How did we ever get here? We have no idea what people are saying… and the Irish seem to talk so fast…using words and phrases that neither one of them could understand.*

After unpacking, Linnea realized that she was starved! When she went down to dinner she was glad to find mounds of potatoes, fish and some overcooked vegetables. She had no idea the Irish ate fish but then she realized it was Friday. When Maureen introduced them, she mentioned to the group that she and Frida were looking for work.

"I can take Bridie and one of you to my job" Maureen offered, "but I don't think I can have the tree of ya."

Then a young woman by the name of Mary spoke up and said, "One of ye can come with me. We have so much work to do, it would be good to have an extra pair of hands…one of ye can help me with the ironing…I'll tell you these people go through laundry like there's no tomorrow."

Early the next morning, Linnea walked to catch a trolley with Bridie and Maureen. It was a cool morning and Linnea was excited to see more of the city. She still wasn't sure where she was and what was the difference between Boston, Cambridge and Somerville. They all seemed to be one place since you could get anywhere on the streetcar with a nickel in your pocket. Maureen had called the streetcar, "the poor man's train." After they had walked the same six blocks back to what Maureen called "Parter Square," they took a streetcar down Mass Ave toward Harvard Square.

They got off the trolley and walked another few blocks to Brattle Street where the houses got larger and farther apart. Some of the homes reminded Linnea of houses built around the spa in Ronneby. *The gardens are beautiful but not quite as grand as those at Ronneby*, Linnea thought. *I am amazed at how this 15-minute ride on the trolley can take you out of a neighborhood where people are packed like sardines to such elegant parks and gracious houses.*

They walked a few blocks through leafy tree-lined Cambridge streets paved with red brick. Soon Maureen stopped before a house that was set back from the street. She motioned them to follow her down a side path to the rear of the house; at the back door, they went down to the scullery and laundry rooms.

"Well, let's get started," said Maureen, as she threw them each an apron. "Here's how we do it. Since it's Saturday, we collect the sheets and big towels. We do those first, so they can dry on Sunday. But first let me light the copper so we can begin the soak." Walking over to a big pile of sheets and towels that the upstairs maid had thrown on the floor, she motioned them over and said, "Here help me with these…you know lifting heavy laundry out of boiling water is a wicked hard job and I'm going to need all the help I can get."

After the sheets and towels had boiled, Maureen stood on the step in front of the built-in copper vat and, with the help of the two girls, lifted the clothes out and into a draining rack with a long dolly stick.

Maureen pointed to a square basket and told them, "This affair is called a mangle. We let clothes dry a while, and then the two of you have to help pull the mangle forward. Then you take this over to the big rinsing tubs and tip the clothes in. The clothes need at least three rinses before putting to drain and then they are rung through on the hand mangle for drying."

"Tomorrow, Sunday, the dirty clothes will be put into piles for us. This'll save time for the main wash on Monday when we'll put the very "darty" kitchen towels and dusters into tubs to soak with some soda and dried soap. I'm glad you'll be here to help with the rest of the hand washing, boiling, rinsing and starching. It's most of a day's work all right."

Around six o'clock, the three women walked back to the trolley stop. Linnea was bone-tired. She had never seen so much wash. Her arms were sore from all of the heavy lifting of the wet sheets and towels, but as they approached the boardinghouse Linnea thought of Nils...*I wonder how he is getting on in North Cambridge?*

By Tuesday, they were washing woolens and flannels and in the afternoon the damp clothing would be folded ready for mangling next day. Wednesday they mangled. As soon as washing dried it was ironed. There was a special ironing room with built-in tables all the way around the walls and a large stove for heating the irons. The ironing lasted Wednesday, Thursday and Friday. On Friday afternoon, clothes were folded and sorted into baskets. At the end of the week, they cleaned and scrubbed out the laundry and the ironing rooms to get ready for Saturday. By Sunday, Linnea was exhausted.

Bridie, who seemed to have endless energy, was also glad to have the afternoon off.

After a couple of weeks of this routine, Linnea decided that on her next Sunday afternoon off she would take a walk around the neighborhood. She had been so tired at the end of each day that she still had no idea of where she was living. The daily routine had been to get up at 5:00 A.M., take the trolley to Harvard Square, work in the laundry, come home for dinner and fall into bed to sleep until the next morning.

SEVEN

Taking the Right Turn

When Sunday came, the weather was hot and humid and Linnea decided that she needed to get out and see the neighborhood. Walking up the hill, she took a right onto Summer Street. After a couple of blocks, she decided to take another right and go down Linden Street. The name reminded her of the linden trees at home and of all the "Linds" she had known…Lindquists, Lindbergs, names that tumbled before her. Soon she was lost in thought…so much so, that she didn't notice a young man who was coming out of a lane off of Linden Street. Suddenly, she heard her name. "Linnea, Linnea…what good luck!" It was Nils.

Linnea was ecstatic. She couldn't believe it was Nils. She had missed him and had almost given up hope of ever seeing him again. A minute passed before she found her voice.

"So Nils, what have you been up to?”

Nils tried to hide his surprise at Linnea appearing just a few steps short of his boarding house but nervously blurted out, "Well I live just up the lane here and I have found some work making picture frames in a shop up on Broadway here in Somerville. Do you live around here?"

His deep baritone voice was like music to her. It was a voice that she had longed to hear and for the first time, she realized that she was lonely. "Well, for a short while I'm staying at Harvard Place, a few blocks from here. Bridie and her sister have found me work in a big house in Cambridge. We do the laundry. This is my afternoon off."

Nils couldn't take his eyes off her. Her thick auburn hair piled atop her head was an elegant frame for the fine features of her face. *A Titian beauty*, he thought. She had lovely color in her cheeks and a smile that had now turned into a broad grin. He was so glad to see that her eyes had that familiar glint of mischief and she seemed happy to see him.

Linnea could feel his scrutiny and quickly tried to break the silence. "So, should we take a walk, maybe have a coffee?" she said laughing, as she held out her hand. When Nils took her hand in his and smiled, she felt like she had come home.

That was the beginning of many walks they took around the neighborhood of Spring Hill in Somerville. Nils courted

Linnea for the next year and a half until it was clear to both of them that they would marry. But before it could happen, they had to continue to work and save for that day. Nils worked as a frame-maker for a talented woodcarver who produced frames for leading artists such as John Singer Sargent. He also taught violin and occasionally played for the Boston Pops when they needed a substitute. Linnea continued to work as a live-in maid in a widow's house on Harvard Lane.

Boarding house where Nils lived.

In March of 1912, Nils and Linnea married and moved into rooms at 10 Olive Street, a house across the street from Nils's boarding house. They hadn't saved enough, but a baby was on the way and they were looking forward to a long life together. On August 29, 1912, Linnea walked to the Somerville Hospital and gave birth to a daughter, Sigrid Silvia Christina Vensberg. Nils, who by then had tired of Wansberg being pronounced with a "W" and not a "V'" had changed his name to Vensberg.

10 Olive Street in Somerville

The first four years in America was certainly a period of adjustment to their new surroundings, but all things considered it was a welcome change in comparison to what Nils and Linnea had left behind in Sweden. Nils had settled into a comfortable lifestyle supported by the friendship of his sister

85

Gerda and her husband Gustav. Likewise, Linnea had her sister Frida and her affable Scottish husband John. Nils had also developed a sizeable community of friends from work. They were all from diverse ethnic backgrounds and shared the goal of searching for a better set of circumstances than those they had left.

He missed his family back in Sweden but their weekly letters kept him well informed and their content actually helped reinforce his belief that he had made the right choice in coming to America.

They wrote about the conditions that led to the outbreak of World War One in 1914. Sweden had maintained a firm position of neutrality, but the conflict still had a profound effect on its economy. Even though the first two years of the war proved to be a trading boom, especially with respect to goods flowing to Germany, the government was compelled to impose a heavy "war boom tax" on industry profits. The revenue from the tax supported a newly activated military that was forced to protect Sweden's borders and waterways.

Nils worried constantly about his father who was now on active duty along with two of his younger brothers. They would be away from home now for extended periods of time and he was concerned for his mother and sisters who were left alone in the city of Karlstad. In her letters, his mother wrote of their difficult adjustment to the congestion and hurried pace of city life, and how much they missed the peace and quiet of the countryside.

As the war expanded, Sweden's trading boom quickly disappeared. The British blockade and the German U-boat warfare drastically diminished Sweden's foreign imports and exports. Thousands of tons of cargo and more than 800 lives were lost. By 1916, a combination of poor harvests and the extraordinary expense of maintaining military neutrality had a profoundly negative effect on the economy. The government attempted to pay for their growing deficit by printing money, which only caused high inflation. Salary increases lagged far behind the inflationary rate making it difficult to pay for the spiraling price increase for most goods. To make matters worse, food rationing had to be imposed upon an already depressed population.

Meanwhile, in stark contrast, Nils and his family were experiencing a relatively steady improvement in their life style. The United States managed to steer clear of the conflict and was enjoying a manufacturing upswing due to the increased European demand for everything from copper, iron and ball bearings to food and textiles.

Although Nils was working long six-day weeks, his job seemed secure and the U.S. economy in general was fairly stable. Linnea would take in laundry and clean houses for extra money whenever Frida was available to baby-sit for Siri. Together their yearly income was close to nine hundred dollars. This was only slightly below the average wage in America at the time and they were able to save a small amount each month and enjoy an occasional minor splurge, even though it was usually spent on food.

There were many amazing differences between the "Old Country" and America, but the item that topped the list was food. They had both grown up with a steady, unattractive, never-ending diet of oatmeal porridge, potatoes, hard rye bread and fish. Their food had been fairly substantial but hardly ever varied. Even though Nils was brought up on a farm, fresh eggs and the occasional rabbit, deer or wild turkey shot by his father were the only relief from what was a very basic diet.

Due to the lack of refrigeration, milk was generally in the form of buttermilk or sour milk that was eventually churned into butter or cheese to stretch the resource even further. Only during Christmas did they allow themselves a special treat of rice pudding with cinnamon. Vegetables were rare, and fresh fruit almost non-existent.

In Boston, however, open markets provided them with an unbelievable array of meats, fresh vegetables, fish and fruit that they had only been able to read about until now. For Nils and Linnea, a trip to the market was an event filled with great anticipation. Who could have imagined a dozen oranges for 13 cents, fresh milk at 36 cents per gallon, bread for 7 cents a loaf and something called Campbell's soup; three cans for 25 cents? There was beef, pork, lamb and a wide variety of fish, many of which, to Linnea's surprise, were familiar to her. She would never leave the market without taking home a generous amount of herring, pickled with dill weed from the large oak barrels of the fishmonger.

In what little free time Nils had, he managed to give violin lessons and sing with the Swedish Choral Society. Music was his passion and singing was just one of his many creative pursuits.

EIGHT

Small Pleasures

Linnea had none of the fears that usually plague new mothers. True to form, she took charge and didn't give a thought to what she assumed was a natural event. Three of her seven siblings were younger than her and it was a given that the older children looked after the younger. With Siri in tow, she also managed to help Frida with her new baby who was born prematurely. Aileen was only two pounds at birth and Frida, who was terrified of handling this fragile baby, asked for her sister's help. Fearless, Linnea took over the care of tiny Ailleen. Putting the baby in a large bread pan that she had lined with soft towels soaked in oil, Linnea set it on the open door of a warm oven to regulate the baby's temperature. Aileen thrived. In her own way, Linnea had successfully created a neonatal unit in her own kitchen! When Astrid, Nils and Linnea's second daughter was born on February 19, 1914, tiny Aileen was a healthy one-year-old.

However, while Linnea was busy creating order in her family's life, the rest of the world was in chaos. On May 1, 1915, German U-boats sank the Lusitania off the coast of Queenstown, Ireland. It was a major development at the time. Many speculated that it was done solely with the intent to draw the United States into the war. Although the majority of the passengers that perished were Europeans returning home from holiday or business in America, there were one hundred and twenty four Americans on board as well.

Nils normally did not buy a daily newspaper, even at the price of two cents per copy. However, he couldn't help but notice the small young boy carrying several copies of the Boston Globe under his arm who yelled, "Lusitania sunk by German U-boat! 124 Americans die…read all about it!" Nils managed to grab a copy that was left on a bench, most probably by someone in a hurry to catch the trolley. Sitting down, he began to look at the large picture on the front page. It was the Lusitania…ablaze and sinking into the Atlantic off the coast of Ireland. Turning the page, he found a listing of the passengers that were presumed dead or missing and hoped that he wouldn't find someone he might know from Sweden.

He was relieved when he didn't find any Swedish names

he recognized but when he got to the list of crewmembers one name in particular stood out from all the rest. It was that of Harold Robbins, the steward who served as his daily escort to the dining hall while aboard the Saxonia. This was the same man who magically transformed himself from a prejudiced and aloof adversary into an understanding and genuinely warm-hearted soul in the few days that it took to cross the Atlantic Ocean. He suspected that Robbins was a common name in England, but Nils had a strong premonition that this was the same man he came to know as a friend. He didn't know why or how Harold had found himself aboard the Lusitania, especially at such an ill-fated and inopportune time, but he just knew it was he.

As it turns out, Nils never discovered whether it really was Harold or not, but in reality his intuition was correct. When the war began the Saxonia was requisitioned by the government and pulled from commercial service. It was used as a troopship and also as accommodation for German prisoners of war. Most of the crew on the Saxonia was replaced with military personnel. Due to his long service with the Cunard Line, Harold was offered a Chief Steward's position on board the Lusitania. One year later he would find himself at the wrong end of a torpedo.

Nils didn't have an opportunity to read the daily newspaper very often so he continued to flip through the pages. In the section titled "SPORTS" he noticed the headline, "RED SOX WIN AGAIN AS RUTH PITCHES 2 HITTER". Nils didn't know much about baseball except that fame was usually fleeting in professional sports. As he read on, he learned that this man with the peculiar name, Babe Ruth was only twenty years old. Nils figured the young Mr. Ruth had better enjoy the notoriety while it lasted. Surely he would be gone from the newspaper headlines in another two or three years. Nils speculated that maybe he should try to become a hitter. He remembered hearing some of his co-workers discussing how a good hitter would often times make twice the amount of a pitcher.

The article frequently referred to the Boston Red Sox as the "World Champions", which thoroughly confused Nils since he knew of no baseball teams in the rest of the world. Sweden certainly didn't have one! Apparently they had also won something called the "World Series" several years in a row. Again, he wondered how many other baseball teams in the world existed and how they all got together for this championship.

He tucked the newspaper under his arm, in anticipation of showing the news to Linnea, and headed back to the apartment. When he arrived home, Nils found little Astrid asleep on the couch and Siri, who was now three, sitting at the small wooden dining table being fed some white beans and pork by her mother. He could smell the freshly baked bread that must have just come out of the oven. Linnea gave Nils a tired but warm smile as he closed the front door.

Their living quarters seemed to be closing in, now that there were four of them, and the stress and strain of taking care of two little ones, in addition to taking in laundry for extra money, was beginning to show on Linnea's face. It was not so much the size of the apartment, as they had both come from large families living in small spaces, but the fact that the city of Boston had become so overcrowded during the previous five years that there seemed to be nowhere to get a sense of escape…especially during the long dreary winter months.

The winters were hard for Linnea. She was fatigued and seemed to catch every cold that came around. She had a cough that never seemed to go away. Nils, concerned about her health and their cramped quarters, decided it would be good to move to western Massachusetts where it was less densely populated. Another child was on the way and Nils was worried about the outbreak of influenza in Massachusetts. The deadly virus had arrived in Boston's port on a ship from Europe and by September 1918, thousands of people in Massachusetts were dying of "Spanish Flu" or "La Grippe" as it was called. Already, thousands of American soldiers were suffering from this epidemic in France. Nils was anxious to move the family west and out of the densely populated Boston area. With the establishment of the streetcar lines, Somerville's suburban growth and population had exploded, growing six fold between 1870 and 1915.

Painting and frame by Nils Vensberg

The decision to move was a hard one for Nils. Boston was a great environment for him. He relished the concerts and the many friends he had in the Swedish Choral Society. Even his work as a frame maker was going well. Since the turn of the century, the art of frame making in Boston was having a renaissance. Nils had been at the right place at the right time. He was able to exploit his skills in woodcarving while still finding some time for his passion—painting landscapes of the country he had left behind.

The Prendergast brothers and Hermann Dudley Murphy were the leading frame makers at the time. It was their exquisite carving and gilding skills in executing frame designs that made Boston a center of American frame making.

The Arts and Crafts movement was strong in and around Boston in the late 1890s. When Murphy began carving and gilding frames in the basement of his Winchester, MA home, he had named his frame shop Carrig-Rohane, Gaelic for Red Cliff. He moved his shop into Boston in 1905 and formed a partnership with Swedish-born master carver Walfred Thulin. In 1907, Murphy and Thulin's work was exhibited in the Copley Hall exhibition in Boston. It was the beginning of featuring hand-made frames as a distinct art form. Carrig-Rohane soon was producing frames from designs by leading artists Frederick Childe Hassam and William Merritt Chase for their paintings.

Fortunately, Nils discovered that Walfred Thulin was also from Karlstad. He had met Thulin on a few occasions and admired his work. Nils had a hunch that if anybody knew of a job outside the city, it would be him. After talking to a number of the contacts that Thulin gave him, Nils found work in Springfield, Massachusetts. Located ninety miles west of Boston, Springfield, at the time, was the cultural center of what was called the Pioneer Valley. In 1912, a stunning Italian Renaissance library had opened that was funded by the citizens of Springfield and philanthropist, Andrew Carnegie. The magnificent building of granite, marble and terra cotta had collections of books, paintings, objects of scientific interest, maps and drawings, and sculpture. On the same quadrangle where the library was built, there was also an "Art Museum" in the style of an Italian villa with grand gallery space and room to house various collections.

Although he was reluctant to leave these exciting times in Boston where frame making was being considered an important art form, Nils always put his family first. He was encouraged by the fact that Springfield was a community that supported the arts. In November 1917, Nils, Linnea and their two children piled their belongings onto a train and headed for Springfield. In June of the next year, their son, John William Vensberg was born.

NINE

Moving On

When confronted with a problem Nils had a very methodical and disciplined way of reaching a solution. He was never prone to making snap decisions, but rather he would devour as much information from books, professionals, friends or whomever he trusted to provide an honest opinion on the subject at hand. Linnea, of course, was the person he trusted the most and always the most influential in his decision process. It was easy for him to talk with his wife and there was little he would not share with her.

The children were put to bed routinely after supper at 7:30 P.M. and usually fell asleep to a soft violin serenade from Nils. Playing the violin, served to comfort the children as they dozed off, but it also afforded Nils some practice keeping his fingers nimble after a long day of wood carving at the shop.

Once the children were put to sleep, he and Linnea would enjoy an hour or so of lively conversation about anything and everything that came to mind. It was an opportunity to relax and revert to speaking Swedish. They tried to speak only English in front of the children. Conversation in any language, whether it be with friends, neighbors, co-workers or the merchants at the local market was a treasured form of entertainment. It was as important to them as music, a long leisurely walk or a good meal.

Nils felt it was a good time to bring up something that had been bothering him. They had talked about the subject before, but today, Nils had decided to deal with what had been bothering him for months…now there was no stopping him. "You know Linnea", he began, "this cough of yours is not getting any better and I have been thinking that it's time that we do something about it. The doctor who delivered John seemed like a very competent man and someone we can trust. I think we should see him as soon as possible…before whatever you have, gets any worse."

There were times when Linnea would challenge Nils, gently proposing an alternative perspective, but this was not one of those opportunities. She had become progressively more concerned about her health and especially how it might affect the children. It was almost a relief to her that Nils was trying to bring the issue to a head. "Nils", she responded wearily, "I have to admit you are right. I haven't had the strength or energy to even think about what we should do about my condition, but somehow we have to make the time and save whatever money we need to pay the doctor. I worry about the children and the fact that I might be inadvertently infecting them with something."

"Then that is that," Nils said with a tone of finality as he slapped both knees before standing up. "I will stop by Dr. Baker's office tomorrow to make an appointment and we will get to the bottom of this…not to worry."

She could tell he was attempting to be comforting, and was grateful for the effort, but she felt the uncertainty in his voice. Sensing her discomfort, Nils tried to assure her, "With some help, it won't be long before you'll be back to your old self, but for now we both need some rest. It's almost 8:30… we should get to bed." Linnea was relieved; her daily routine of waking at 4:30 in the morning to make bread and breakfast would begin only too soon.

Linnea's usual resilience in "making do" was wavering. With three small children, the effort of moving to a new place, even though the new apartment on Sullivan Street in Springfield was larger and had a small garden, had left her exhausted. She found herself missing the company and friendship of Frida who helped her by taking care of the children on the occasional afternoon. Frida was the only one she could talk to about her failing health. She didn't want to worry Nils…he had enough work to do to keep the family going. The U.S. had entered the war, which meant food was rationed and money was tight so Linnea kept silent about how very tired she was. But Nils had already guessed that she wasn't well and she dreaded the doctor's appointment that Nils had made for her. It wasn't like her to complain but she didn't feel like telling a doctor her problems.

However, the next week she went with Nils and the children to visit Dr. Baker. He examined her and she caught his look of concern when he listened to her chest. She couldn't find the words to ask him what was the matter and it wasn't until they got home that Nils took her aside and tried to explain what was making her feel so tired and weak. She heard the word tuberculosis and felt faint. This was a disease that everyone was talking about. Some of the wealthy women that she had worked for had been afflicted and had lain about for months in bedrooms with the windows open even in the winter. Fresh air was thought to be the cure. People had even built porches on their houses where they slept all year round. It was a disease that everyone was afraid of catching and often patients who were diagnosed were sequestered. Linnea had seen pictures in the paper of women who were confined to tents outside their houses. For the first time in her life Linnea was afraid—afraid of infecting her children, afraid of leaving them without a mother, and afraid of being isolated from Nils.

The news of Linnea's affliction, although devastating enough by itself, was only one of many concerns facing Nils and his family. The U.S. had entered World War One in the spring of 1917 causing fuel shortages, food rationing and a general national feeling of uncertainty. President Wilson designated Herbert Hoover as U.S. Food Administrator, and he initiated a voluntary program of food rationing. Wheatless Wednesdays and meatless Mondays became promotional buzzwords, as the country tried to ensure sufficient food supplies for the armies of the U.S. and their allies. It was considered unpatriotic not to comply with the President's plan and most of the populous sacrificed more than if the plan had been mandatory. Concurrently, the influenza epidemic was sweeping the country, killing more than 600,000 Americans before it was finally brought under control.

The sum of these conditions along with the concern for three small children would be enough to throw most men into panic, despair and self-pity—but not Nils. Always moving forward, he had no time to fall into the "why me" syndrome. He tried to be calm and disciplined as he pursued a solution.

His most reliable and immediate source of information was Dr. Baker. Nils had first met Dr. Baker during the pregnancy of their third child, John William, who later was called Billy. Since then they had developed a strong personal relationship in which there was mutual respect for their scholastic interests. It didn't hurt that he was especially fond of Linnea's homemade bread, which was always given to him after a house call at the Vensbergs.

During the early part of the 20th century most Americans were still leery of a medical practitioner's expertise and probably with good reason. Many of the so-called doctors were poorly trained—most with less than four years of a college education. The profession was yet to be strictly regulated and many medical doctors completed only a couple of years of training before applying for and, unfortunately, receiving a certificate to practice medicine provided that they were able to pay for the nominal licensing fee. The medical profession in Europe, however, was considerably more advanced so Nils was not as skeptical about seeking the advice of a physician. In keeping with his meticulous nature, Nils would canvass his most trusted friends for recommendations and was well prepared to ask the right questions of Dr. Baker during their first meeting. He was relieved when Dr. Baker showed him his Bachelor of Science degree from Boston

University and his medical degree from the same institution four years later.

It was not only the education that convinced Nils of Dr. Baker's competence, however, but also his relaxed, common sense approach to the medical profession. Most of all, Nils appreciated the fact that he was never condescending or patronizing when he talked about medical procedures, diagnosis or theory. He always made Nils feel extremely comfortable in his presence, recognizing that he had a level of inquisitiveness and understanding that allowed him to share more information than he normally would give patients.

Like most doctors of that era, Dr. Baker spent the majority of his time on house calls. He would not return to his small office, which was located inside his residence on the south side of Springfield, until late in the evening. Nils started to make a habit of stopping by to visit after work to discuss Linnea's condition and what medical options were available.

One of the first things Dr. Baker had to explain to Nils was that although the medical term for Linnea's disease was called, tuberculosis, he would often hear it called, "consumption". This was a rather loose term used to describe a variety of illnesses with the common symptoms of general wasting away, loss of weight and ashen skin color. He told Nils not to be fooled by the term consumption because most people used it as an all-inclusive branding of ailments that may or may not include tuberculosis. Secondly, Doctor Baker told Nils that he took the approach of being brutally honest in his description of any disease, the recommended treatment and overall prognosis. There was no point, he said, in sugarcoating the situation and unfairly, leaving the patient and family poorly prepared to deal with the eventual consequences.

Doctor Baker gave Nils some historical background starting with a Dr. Henry Bowditch, an influential Boston physician, who during the 1860's promoted a theory that locale and climate were major causes of consumption. He told Nils that New England physicians discovered what seemed to be a significant correlation between the incidences of consumption, the site of a house, poorly drained soil and dampness. Dr. Baker went on to explain to Nils that Bowditch's recommendation for fresh air, nourishing food, sunshine and avoidance of stress was the prescription followed by most physicians even then in 1920. Statistics for the inmates of Massachusetts's jails before the turn of the century provided further evidence for the theory. The crowded, damp, and unventilated conditions of these jails produced an unusually high incidence of consumption. From 1880 until 1900 no prisoners sentenced to life in the Boston system completed more than twelve years of their sentence; they all succumbed to some form of tuberculosis.

Nils would write as fast as he could and kept copious notes of his interviews with Dr. Baker. In his small notebook he would jot down, in short hand, the details of everything the doctor had to say. Short hand was just another of the varied skills that he had learned in Sweden. He used the technique to communicate with his brother who still remained in the homeland. His plan was to write everything down during his search and sort through it all later, sifting out re-commendations that he considered irrelevant or beyond his monetary means.

Dr. Baker continued by warning Nils about the many home remedies and patent medicines offered by drug stores, street peddlers and even some physicians. Most of these so-called "patent" medicines were not really patented at all and contained high percentages of alcohol, cocaine or opium. One of the more popular remedies of the day was "Dr. Hotstetters Stomach Bitters" which contained 45% alcohol compared to the 40% found in vodka, whiskey and gin. Most of the young men found it easier to buy a bottle of "Dr. Hotsetters" at the drug store for a night out on the town rather than visit a saloon that sold only beer.

One of Dr. Baker's favorites, however, was the popular "Lydia E. Pinkham's Vegetable Compound" advertised widely on the back of newspapers and magazines as an elixir that would cure all sorts female maladies. Dr. Baker had a good laugh with Nils as he explained that most women who abhorred alcohol, and were in fact fervent supporters of the Woman's Temperance Movement, swore by the magical curative effects of "Lydia Pinkham's Vegetable Compound". Dr. Baker leaned over close to Nils and said, "Little do they know that this silly stuff contains 15% alcohol." He leaned back in his chair and with a wry smile on his face said, "No wonder they feel so good! With a healthy shot of that stuff they could probably walk the streets all day long holding their placards up high denouncing the evils of alcohol." For emphasis, he added, "They may not march in a straight line mind you, but march all day they certainly could."

Dr. Baker abruptly stood up from behind his desk and announced, "Well Nils, I think we should continue our discussion another day. In any event, all this talk of alcohol has made me thirsty. How about we open up that bottle of Aquavit you gave me last week?" he said, as he drew out the bottle, appropriately enough, from his office medicine cabinet. "No harm in a shot or two amongst friends", he said, as he poured out two very full shot glasses of the clear liquid.

The long dark winters in Sweden drove many of his countrymen to habitual drinking in order to cope with depressing conditions. It had become something of a national crisis. Nils, however, had managed to avoid falling into this habit. He was not opposed to having an occasional drink, however, and neither was Linnea, for that matter. She was always a step ahead of the so-called "accepted" feminine mores of the day and after they had put the children to bed, it was not unusual for them to share some brandy once or twice a week during their evening talks. They both had seen first-hand the ravaging effects of alcoholism in Sweden. Many of their countrymen chose alcohol as a way of escaping the harsh reality of the long, dark, never ending winters, the bland routine of Scandinavian life and the increasing poverty surrounding them. Both vowed never to succumb to this debilitating practice and managed to hold each other in check. The love they had for each other and their family had always been enough to keep them focused and centered. They never truly found a need to escape from reality. Life, as they knew and lived it, was perfectly satisfying in every way possible.

Eager to get back to the family, Nils pulled out his pocket watch and determined that he would stay only another half-hour with the Doctor and then must start on his way home. As they lifted their glasses in unison, Dr. Baker pronounced, "Here's to making the right choice", as they both downed their shots in one quick swallow.

Over the next half-hour they engaged in some light conversation about Boston, the end of the war, the economy and whatever else came to mind. Nils found it extremely easy to talk with his newfound friend. After the second shot of Aquavit was poured, however, Dr. Baker noticed Nils nervously check his pocket watch for the third time, and he decided to end the conversation with one final thought.

"You know Nils", he said, leaning over and looking him squarely in the eye, "I am going to schedule a number of tests for Linnea and your family over the next few weeks. Depending on the results I will give you my very best professional analysis for a recommended course of treatment…but in the end it will be you who makes the final decision. I can provide you with all of the latest medical information and I will give you as many reasonable alternatives as possible, but the direction you take will be yours. The best piece of advice I can give you in this regard, however, is that once you make the decision don't ever look back, don't ever doubt yourself or it will haunt you forever. You have to convince yourself and Linnea that the course of action you take is absolutely and positively the best possible choice. I have to tell you Nils, the most important personal discovery I've made, over the many years of my medical practice, is that mental health and physical health somehow seem to feed off each other. A positive attitude seems to be a prerequisite for disease prevention and recovery."

Finally he said, "The one thing I do know, Nils, is that we don't have much time. The sooner you make your decision the better and I would put a timetable of no more than three weeks. We are fortunate that Linnea appears to be in the early stages of the disease, but that advantage will quickly disappear if we fail to take action soon."

TEN

Following the Sun

Over the next two weeks Dr. Baker scheduled appointments for the entire Vensberg family. Physical exams, saliva analysis and whatever other medical diagnostic tools available at the time were performed on all of the family members. Nils and Linnea were familiar with most of the tests. However, there was one additional test called an "x-ray" or fluoroscope that amazed them both. Somehow this machine was able to take a fuzzy but yet discernable picture of their bones and insides, bypassing the external features of their face and body they were used to seeing in normal photographs. Dr. Baker explained that this was the very latest medical advancement and it had quickly proven to be particularly effective in the treatment of tuberculosis.

Nils visited Dr. Baker on a regular basis and was even

allowed to look at some of the saliva samples under a high-powered lens called a "microscope" that the doctor had recently purchased for his office. Nils was amazed to discover a whole new world of life under the surface of the skin that he never knew existed. Nils listened intently as Dr. Baker explained the new "germ theory" that many medical scholars were promoting as the wave of the future. They believed that this new world of tiny creatures was responsible for many, if not all, of the maladies suffered by mankind. They felt that if they could learn how to control them or eliminate them, they could begin to fight all sorts of ailments that for centuries had no remedy.

The costs for these tests would normally be out of Nils's financial reach, but Dr. Baker considered Nils a very close friend by now and managed to pull in favors from his colleagues at the hospital. Most of the fees were reduced or waived entirely as Dr. Baker was a well-respected practitioner in the Boston area. In spite of his colleagues' urgings that he pursue a medical specialty, he was perfectly comfortable with the family practice that allowed him to develop personal relationships with members of his immediate community. He enjoyed the home visits and personal touch that seemed to be a remedy in and of itself for those who welcomed him into their homes.

Nils, while appreciative of the doctor's generosity, did everything he could to pay his own way. He contributed as much as he could from his weekly earnings, did minor repairs to the doctor's home, fashioned an ornate wooden shingle for his office and, of course, invited the doctor for countless home-cooked meals at the Vensberg home. Last but not least, a fresh loaf of Linnea's home baked bread was dropped off early each morning at the doctor's doorstep on Nils's way to work.

During this period of lab tests and physical exams, the doctor prescribed plenty of fresh air, sunshine and as much rest as possible for Linnea. There was not much more he could do since there were less than ten medicines that were considered effective for treatment of any disease, cold or flu at the time. Despite Dr. Baker's continuing warning to Nils about the use of "patent medicines", street vendor magical cures and drug store remedies, there was one readily available liquid that he did recommend…cod liver oil. Cod liver oil was an excellent source of vitamin D, the very same vitamin the human body processes from exposure to the sun. Most manufacturers of this thick, foul tasting liquid promoted it as "Sunshine in a bottle".

The medical community was just beginning to realize that there was some correlation between the sunshine states

(Arizona, California and New Mexico) and a reduced incidence of tuberculosis. Dr. Baker prescribed a diet leaning towards other sources of vitamin D such as milk and cheese in addition to fresh vegetables that would give Linnea a healthy supplement of vitamins and minerals. The whole family followed the same eating regimen…there was no time to fix separate meals for each member. The children didn't mind the extra milk and cheese, but the never-ending vegetables coupled with a morning and evening spoonful of cod liver oil bordered on the traumatic. Just the sight of the cod liver oil bottle was enough to make the kids squint their eyes, wrinkle up their noses and bring tears to their eyes. Little Billy was running out of hiding places. It was a two-man job when they did find him; one to hold his arms and the other to pinch his nose shut forcing his mouth to open. Quickly, a large spoonful was administered and a reverse move was accomplished by releasing the pinch on his nose while almost simultaneously covering his mouth to prevent him from spitting it out. It demanded the hand-eye coordination of a professional athlete!

Over the next several days, the decision that Nils had to make was becoming more obvious. None of the conditions required to give Linnea a chance at recovering—fresh air, plenty of sunshine and a rural, sparsely populated living area—could be found in their area. It occurred to him that the damp, dark, cold and densely populated Boston area might have caused Linnea to contract tuberculosis in the first place. Even if he could afford the fancy sanitariums in the Boston area, they all required that the patients be isolated from their families for extended periods of time. This simply was not an option as far as Nils was concerned. The stress on the family, and on Linnea in particular, would negate any benefit a sanitarium could provide. The mere thought of not being able to see Linnea, even for one day, sent a tremendous wave of sadness over him. They had literally never been apart for more than a few hours at a time since their marriage. *We must make a move,* thought Nils, *but where?* Then it occurred to him that he did know someone who could point him in the right direction…his good friend, Lars Magnusson.

ELEVEN

A Decision Is Made

Nils had first met Lars as a fellow member of the Swedish Choral Society. Their group practiced every other Sunday afternoon and usually performed the in-between Sundays at churches and local gatherings around the Boston area. Lars was a huge man by any standard of the day, standing six four and weighing the better part of two hundred and forty pounds. The work boots he wore around the docks as an engine mechanic added another two inches and made him an extremely impressive sight, especially in this era when a man of six feet was considered very tall. Lars had a full sandy blonde beard with a shaggy, unkempt crop of hair of the same color. His large, round and ruddy face completed the image. Indeed, if you were to look up the definition of "Swede" in the dictionary, there would be a picture of Lars. He just needed a helmet and sword to look like a true Viking.

You would surely expect a man of Lars' size to be the anchor of the choir with a big deep bass voice. But Lars, in this respect, was one of life's strange incongruities. What came out of his mouth was a beautiful tenor. It always amazed Nils to hear the clear delicate tone of this voice coming out of such an enormous man.

Lars had come to America five years prior to Nils in 1905. Since the age of seventeen, he had worked as a master mechanic for a large fishing fleet in Gotenberg. Much like Nils, he was a product of the Swedish craftsman system, beginning as an apprentice, then served as journeyman until finally achieving status as a master mechanic. His mother had died when he was only four after succumbing to complications following a bout with pneumonia. His father was lost at sea in1904 when Lars was twenty. He was left with virtually no family and he became somewhat of a loner.

Working in a port town afforded him many opportunities to travel. His good reputation as a mechanic was well known in Gotenberg and there were several offers from the captains of the many foreign freighters that brought merchandise to Gotenberg from Europe and occasionally, America. After his father's death he finally decided to accept an offer from the German cargo ship line of Brindenberg. He managed to make a few trips to America where he was often pressed into service, on loan so to speak, to give his advice on various mechanical problems aboard passenger steamships. While docked in the ports of Boston or New York, Lars's captain would invariably find that one of his colleagues, usually a drinking partner, was in need of some mechanical assistance for his ship. One of the steamship companies, The Savannah Line, was so impressed with his talent that they offered to sponsor him for immigration to America if he would accept a position with them. Lars didn't accept immediately, but finally on his next voyage to America, he decided to abandon his sea legs and accept an offer from The Savannah Line.

Nils found Lars on the dock of the Boston Terminal, Pier 42 of the Hoosac Tunnel Docks. Lars had attempted to wipe the grease off his oversized hand before extending it to Nils, but it was a futile effort. Nils, gripping his oil-soaked hand, went right to the point. Lars listened intently with a look of deep concern on his face as Nils began to describe Linnea's illness in great detail. Lars was not a well-educated man, and didn't fully understand the medical terminology and treatments available at the time. But he did understand the brutal reality of what had happened to his close friend and family. The entire ordeal left him with a complete sense of helplessness. It was uncomfortable for him to hear and feel the sense of desperation in Nils's voice. They had been close friends for a long time and he had always found Nils to be extremely resilient and optimistic, especially in the face of difficult times when money or job security was in question. Those problems he could easily understand, but what Nils was describing to him was completely different. He sensed Nils's desperation. He knew his good friend was in trouble and was at odds as to how he could help...it was only when Nils mentioned the need to leave the Boston area for a better climate that he interrupted him and said,

"I have an idea!"

He began to tell Nils how his company, The Savannah Line, was going through a tremendous upswing in passenger service to Florida. Lars spoke of ghostly white, lifeless Bostonians boarding ships bound for Florida who would return just two weeks later, relaxed, tan and glowing with new life.

"You should have seen the difference between the returning Florida vacationers and the family and relatives that greeted them at the dock...it was amazing. It's as if they had returned from a wonderful spa."

During the time the United States was involved in World War I, most of the merchant and passenger ships, as well as the trains, were commandeered by the government to transport troops and supplies to New York where they would leave for the conflict in Europe. Although Lars would be kept busy with the maintenance of the seventeen ships the company owned, it was a difficult time for the owners. The ships and trains, however, were returned to their owners following the end of the war in 1918, and the US economy was booming. Many middle-class Americans had money and the time to travel. Paid vacations, pensions, benefits and most importantly the beginning of American's love affair with the car were important benchmarks of the 1920s. Families now had the mobility and the extra cash to invest. Florida beckoned. Land was cheap and a small investment could promise instant wealth. In northern cities, like Boston, the newspapers were full of stories of how land investors doubled their profits in months. The land boom was in full swing in Florida. For Middle America, the opportunity to vacation and prospect for a prime piece of property was an allurement that was difficult to pass up.

Nils's eyes widened and a smile began to slowly wash across his face, as he listened to Lars. While Lars continued to talk about the company ships that sailed for Florida—their speed, dimensions, engine size, propellers, cargo space, etc., Nils was no longer listening. He was already deep in thought, making plans in his head for the trip that he knew the family should take. As Lars continued to drone on with details of double hulls and triple expansion engines, Nils was already envisioning himself on board with Linnea and the children, out on the open sea with the fresh sea air and warm sun beginning to work nature's magic to defeat her disease.

When Lars finished, he had to tap Nils on the shoulder to awaken him from his daydream. "You are a wonderful friend Lars", Nils said as he slowly drifted back into reality. "I think you may have just given me the answer to my problems…do you think you could get me some more information about prices, sailing times and accommodations? I'll need to piece all of this together very soon."

Lars was only too happy to give his promise to find out all the details. He thought he might even be able to get free fares for the children by talking with some employees that owed him favors. The two men shook hands and Nils walked down the Hoosac Tunnel docks with a renewed vigor.

Meanwhile back at home, Linnea who was cleaning up the kitchen realized she was exhausted. Taking care of her three small children had been a challenge and her illness made her feel tired all the time.

I never seem to be able to take a breath, she thought, as she looked at a pile of laundry, which was getting bigger every day. *I can't believe that my friends and I used to do laundry all day...I had so much more energy then. I would love to be where it would be warm all the time...I'll never get rid of this cough with these long and cold winters.* Tired, she sat down and dreamed of the hot sun on her back, sitting in a chair in her own garden.

The moment of calm didn't last for long. Soon the children were pulling on her skirt and asking for lunch. She was glad she had made a big pot of soup the night before but was so tired that she didn't have the energy to do more than cut some bread and turn the heat under the soup.

Linnea heard someone at the front door. She was surprised that it was Nils. Usually he didn't come home until suppertime. Feeling that he had something on his mind, she said, "Sätta sig," sat down at the kitchen table and waited.

Nils pulled out a chair, took her hand and got right to the point. "I just had a nice long visit with Lars...I have some exciting news." He then began to tell her about Lars's description of the Florida vacationers returning to Boston... "Brown as berries and the absolute picture of health."

Linnea's face brightened as she listened to Nils talk about Florida. She enjoyed his enthusiasm and was drawn into his infectious non-stop banter. When he was finished, he said to her, "Linnea, I think we finally have a solution to our problem. I have to admit, over the past several weeks I didn't know what direction to take, but now I think a move to Florida is exactly what we should do. Dr. Baker insists that time is not in our favor and now that we know where to go, we should make plans as soon as possible."

Nils tried to stay calm, he didn't want Linnea to think he might be anxious about this move…even though he wasn't sure what they would find when they got down there. *It couldn't be all that risky*, he thought, *I've been hearing about the land boom in Florida for some months now.*

Feeling the need to keep Linnea's spirits up, he said, "Florida is booming right now…maybe we can get a small piece of land and I'll build a house." Linnea looked at him and gave him a smile that she hoped would reassure him. She knew that this was a good decision and that he was doing this for her. He never stopped worrying about her health. Her only regret was that he would have to give up his music and his craft as a frame-maker for a while…maybe a long while. She also knew Florida was still a wilderness and couldn't imagine how they would survive.

Nils could sense that she was far away in her thoughts. Rather than let the silence lengthen he said, "I know what you're thinking", and then he paused, "if it's about my music and carving just remember they are friendly companions and easy travelers too." Pointing to his head and his heart, he said,

"They both live forever here and here and will always be with me wherever I go. All I need is my violin and I'll be a happy man. Don't worry about a thing. This will all work out for the best. We can trust our good friend Lars to help and just making plans for the trip may be even more fun than the trip itself. The children will have a wonderful time!"

She trusted Nils more than anyone else, so his words were more than enough reassurance for her to relax ever so slightly. In fact, after a long pause between them, she suddenly began to laugh almost uncontrollably. Nils was only too happy to feel the tension breaking, but had to ask what was so funny.

"Oh my goodness Nils, when you mentioned Lars I couldn't help but remember the dinner we had at our American friends, the Altons, after a Swedish Choral Society rehearsal. Mrs. Alton was so gracious to us all, but don't you remember when she asked Lars if he wanted a second helping. Lars said, "No I can't, I'm really fed up with all this food!" Poor Mrs. Alton didn't quite know what to say, until she finally realized the humor in what Lars thought was a way to say, "I'm full.""

It was one of those rare moments when it was almost impossible to stop laughing and Nils was so relieved to see Linnea happy.

Most Americans were prospering, but Nils and Linnea

had only been in the States for eight years and they were still scrambling to make ends meet. Even though Nils didn't have the money to invest in a purely speculative way, he knew that as land prices rose, there would be plenty of work for a skilled carpenter. *After all,* he thought, *someone has to build houses on these properties.*

He had heard of the tent cities that had sprung up around these booming Florida towns and thought that this was their best bet. Travelling by car was becoming so popular that the locals would set up campgrounds for what they called the "Tin Can Tourists." Eager for the fun and sunshine, people would rig up their cars with five-gallon drums of extra water, folding side tents, pack the family in their Model T and head south. If they were investors, they would live in these camps while they built their vacation homes. This new middle class wasn't interested, nor could they afford, the elegant hotels that were being established in the major resort areas like Tampa and Miami. Nils felt they would fit in and would have the company of other families who were trying to establish themselves in this new place.

It would be a relief, he thought, *not to worry about the cold. I can't even imagine being in a place where the weather was balmy and you can pick oranges off the trees.*

The decision to leave was made and the next three weeks

were filled with a whirlwind of planning in anticipation of their impending trip. There was so much to do in such little time. Notices were given to the landlord and Nils's foreman at work, school records collected for Siri, the sale and sometimes donation of their meager amounts of furniture, kitchenware and winter clothes, the purchase of boat tickets to Savannah and then to Tampa by train…the list was endless. Most of these activities were easily accomplished as they checked them off their well-organized list, but there remained two things that would give them brief periods of anxiety about the move, even though Nils and Linnea both agreed that it was an unavoidable consequence of their plight.

The first was taking young Siri out of school where reports from her teachers described a quick learner who was well ahead of her classmates. They had strongly recommended she skip a grade to a level where she would have more of a challenge. But when Siri's first grade teacher heard about the move, she was confident that Nils would nurture her curiosity with the books that he read to her and the family on a regular basis. She knew that his passion for music and the arts would provide an added dimension to her overall education. In spite of this difficult decision, both teacher and parents seem to agree that everyone would profit from the move and that doing their schoolwork at home would be a challenge but something they could manage. Linnea and Nils's efforts would reflect the home-schooling format adopted in the U.S. some seventy years later.

They planned their departure to coincide with the end of the school year in June of 1918. Before they left Boston, however, Linnea wanted to make sure that Siri and Asta were christened in their church. She was concerned that they may not find a church readily in Florida and thought it best to get the christenings done before they left. Despite her illness, Linnea summoned the strength to make the christening dresses for Sigrid and Asta. Arrangements were hastily made and in May the pastor of their Lutheran Church formerly christened the girls.

Another aspect of their plan troubled them. It involved leaving the many close friends and relatives they had in Boston, in particular Linnea's sister, Frida, and Nils's sister, Gerda. They both remembered how difficult it was to leave their families in Sweden only eight years earlier and now to go through a similar event all over again would be very traumatic. They wondered when, or if, they would ever see each other again? Barely coming to grips with the fact that they would probably never return to see their families in Sweden, they now were confronted with the feeling of losing contact with their friends and family in Boston.

Although Frida had adjusted well to family life, and matured immensely as a mother, she would always rely on her older sister's sense of humor and unrelenting zest for life. The

Christening 1918: Siri and Linnea "Asta"

increasing look of despair on Frida's face became evident as their departure grew closer, and Linnea hoped that Gustav and Gerda would remain a source of family support for her.

128

Nils would find it difficult to leave Gustav and Gerda but knew that they would continue to thrive in Boston. They had just bought a house on Marten Street in West Roxbury, and Gustav had a very good job at the local dairy, while Gerda was doing a wonderful job raising their two young sons.

Meanwhile, Lars had made arrangements for their trip by boat to Savannah, Georgia and by train via the Atlantic Coastline Railroad from Savannah to Tampa. Nils regretted leaving Lars and obviously the feeling was mutual since Lars had assumed that they would return and had at first quoted an excursion fare, which was round trip. Nils had to remind poor Lars that the tickets should be one-way, as they would not be returning. The ticket for the steamship portion of the ship was $24.10 each, plus an eight percent wartime tax, which remained in effect even though World War 1 had ended months ago. Each ticket included meals and stateroom accommodations in the intermediate or second-class section of the ship. Although most of the Savannah Line ships had steerage rates, the two ships that serviced the Boston-Savannah route in 1918 only offered first and second class. Linnea and Nils both remembered the dormitory style accommodations in steerage on the Saxonia and looked forward to traveling in relative style this time. The meals would certainly be better than the watered down soup, porridge and stale bread offered by the Saxonia. Fortunately, Lars had also arranged for the three children to travel free, so the grand total for the family trip to Savannah was $52.05. It was a good chunk of their savings but, nonetheless, about a third cheaper than taking the train to Savannah.

They would be traveling aboard the steamship named *The City of Columbus,* a sixteen year-old ship with a much larger capacity for freight than passengers. The cargo area could handle several thousand bales of cotton and several tons of perishable fruit and vegetables. A novel ventilation system allowed the free flow of air entering from the bow and exiting at the stern. This circulating air kept the cargo of fresh fruit and vegetables cool enough to prevent spoilage. There would be one crewmember for every three passengers, so the Vensberg family could expect to be well taken care while on board.

It would take a total of seventy hours to reach Savannah from Boston. It was a relatively short trip, although it could seem like an eternity when trying to keep up with the mischievous non-stop antics of little Billy who was now closer to three but seemed to be still in the phase of the "terrible two's". Linnea could only hope that her two daughters, Siri and Asta would be able to keep track of him.

The day before they were due to leave, Nils paid a final

visit to Dr. Baker to say good-bye and thank him for all of his help. After a relaxed conversation about the impending trip, Dr. Baker pulled open the top drawer of his desk and surprised Nils with a leather bound journal and a small glass thermometer. He sheepishly explained to Nils, "This, my friend, is what I would call a 'boomerang gift' as someday I hope you will return it to me. You see, there is still a great deal that we don't know about tuberculosis", he continued. "It would be of tremendous value for me to follow the progress of Linnea. I would appreciate your efforts to keep daily notes in this journal about her general condition…how frequently she coughs, energy level, redness of the eyes, body soreness, skin color, or anything noticeably different, either good or bad. The thermometer is the only measuring tool I can give you, but if you could record her temperature two or three times per day it would be a big help. When Linnea has fully recovered, and we both know she will, you can send the journal back to me. Who knows, I might even surprise my snooty colleagues with a fancy report in the American Medical Journal. Linnea will be famous!"

As they shook hands for what would probably be the last time, Dr. Baker cautioned Nils, "Remember what I told you. Don't ever look back and second-guess yourself. You've made the right decision."

TWELVE

Pickled Herring

On a bright and warm Saturday afternoon in June of 1918, the Vensberg family boarded the Savannah Line's ship *City of Columbus* for the first leg of their journey to Florida. Moments earlier they had said a tearful good bye to the family of Nils's sister, Gerda and the family of Linnea's sister, Frida. They all had made the trip to Pier 52 of the Hoosac Tunnel Docks on Boston harbor to bid them farewell. Fortunately, Lars had secured a company pass that allowed him to board with Nils and Linnea. He carried Billy in his arms while Nils and Linnea held the hands of Siri and little Asta as they made their way up the wooden gangplank to the main deck of the ship. Lars managed to spend some time showing them around the ship until a steward came by to announce that the ship would be leaving in thirty minutes. Lars gave them all a big bear hug and then he joined Gerda and Frida on the dock where they waved goodbye to the Vensberg family, which by now was standing on the Hurricane deck and waving back. Within minutes of a long blast from the ship's steam horn, the tugboats pulled the *City of Columbus* away from the dock and into the open water of Boston Harbor until it was positioned to move away under its own power.

Linnea, exhausted by the time they boarded the ship, had been totally preoccupied trying to keep track of three small children as well as managing the bulk of all the odds and ends that they needed to set up a new household. She hoped that she hadn't forgotten anything that they would need right away. Nils had reassured her that if they did forget something, they could find what they needed in Tampa/St. Petersburg. That was just some of the information that he had read about in the tent camp's Florida travel guide, "Sun Hunting".

"You know this camp DeSoto Park in Tampa has electric lights, running water, city sewerage, shower baths and an enormous hot-water tank," Nils said. "I think we can be quite comfortable there. The article that I read said that the only things that aren't furnished are free telephones, a free morning paper and a free butler!"

Linnea laughed and said, "Well I think we can manage.... although a free butler would have been nice!" Somehow she was beginning to feel better…she realized that in the chaos of trying to meet the boat and manage all of their belongings, that it was time to enjoy this adventure. Now that they were finally on their way, she sat on deck with the children and watched as Boston slowly disappeared on the horizon.

It seems like such a short time ago that I was just arriving with all kinds of hope for the future, she thought. *Now I am leaving and I have no idea what will come next. I can't even imagine what it will be like to live in a tent.*

It was only a matter of days when she would find out.

As the *City of Columbus* began to weave its way through the islands of the Boston Harbor, Nils patiently pointed out the lighthouse markers along the way to Siri and Asta. There was no radar in 1919, so the light houses that appeared at regular intervals along the coast were essential navigational tools for the captains of the many freight and passenger ships that ran up and down the Atlantic seaboard of the United States. Nils clicked off the lighthouses…first the Boston lighthouse some nine miles away…then the Hardings buoy two and a half miles later…then Minot's light. They would pass more than forty such lighthouse markers on their way to Savannah.

The boat continued to journey across Massachusetts Bay past Provincetown at the tip of Cape Cod where it turned south towards Savannah. During the late afternoon the *City of*

Columbus continued along the arm of Cape Cod and then turned west at Pollock Rip into Nantucket Sound. After a little more than an hour, they entered the narrow channel between Martha's Vineyard and the Elizabeth Islands. They were now approaching an important landmark. Thirty-six years earlier, on January 18, 1884 the first *City of Columbus* was steaming through this same narrow channel when pilot error slammed it into "Devils's Bridge" rocks near the Gay Head lighthouse on Martha's Vineyard. Seventy-five passengers lost their lives in the icy waters that night.

The next morning, when she realized that she was free of her chores, Linnea gently nudged Nils to tell him that she was going to take a walk on deck for a few hours and would return to join them for breakfast.

Unlike her steerage accommodations aboard the Saxonia, she was not restricted to a limited area of the ship. The family would have access to every area of the vessel and Linnea was going to take full benefit of the freedom to roam. Their cabin was located on the main deck at the stern of the ship and as she gently shut the door to their quarters, Linnea walked a short distance down the hall and through doors that led directly onto the aft deck of the *City of Columbus*. Even though it was mid-June, the cool air of the morning breeze was pleasant. Far away she could see the city lights and the stars that shone brightly against the dark sky as the ship moved through the open sea. It had been more than fifteen hours since they had left Boston Harbor and they were now steaming along the coast of Long Island with another ten hours to go before passing the port of New York. As Linnea strolled along the main deck, she worked her way up to the bow of the ship. There, she could see one of the many lighthouses that would guide them along their journey sending a wide beam of white light from the coastline. Once Linnea reached the bow of the ship, she followed the steps up to the Hurricane deck where the staterooms and first class passenger cabins were located. The dining hall, which seated more than seventy-five at one sitting, was positioned on the Hurricane deck, and had a spectacular panoramic view of the ocean over the bow. Peeking through the windows, Linnea could see the dining hall and the crew setting the tables for breakfast.

This was going to be good, she thought, *fresh linen and silver!*

Linnea continued around the Hurricane deck, stopped to open a deck chair from the stack of chairs that were folded up against the wall, and thought w*hat a pleasure,* as the cool ocean air washed over her. *I'll just enjoy the view.*

The only sounds that penetrated the stillness of the night were the slight rumbling of the ship's engines and the soothing splash of water as the ship plowed relentlessly through the Atlantic coastal waters. It was a rare moment alone for Linnea, as she stared out over the open sea. Although she had worrisome thoughts about her illness and what it would portend for their new life in Florida, she wouldn't allow any negative feelings to creep into this special moment. She could only sit still for twenty minutes and then she was up…ready to continue her stroll by the bright full moon that hung low in the sky.

At the end of her walk, she was rewarded with a spectacular sunrise, which reflected the occasional white cap on an unusually calm sea.

Linnea returned to their cabin at 6:00 A.M. to find Nils and the children wide-awake and excitedly preparing for the day. Nils, as always, had a bright smile on his face and was more than pleased to see the relaxed look on Linnea's face as she entered the cabin. Nils took little Billy by the hand and led him down the hall to the bathrooms that were equipped with both seawater and fresh water showers. A shower was something none of the children had experienced before and there was non-stop chatter about the event when Linnea returned from the bathrooms with Nils and little Billy.

When everyone was dressed, they all marched up the stairs to the Hurricane deck and proceeded towards the main dining hall for breakfast. What an unbelievable treat it was for everyone, especially Linnea. Having breakfast prepared and served to her by friendly young men who were immaculately dressed in smart white uniforms was a well-deserved departure from her usual early morning routine. It was a sumptuous meal with refills of fresh coffee and juice, and never-ending fresh pastries for the children. *It is almost too good to be true,* she thought.

During the afternoon, Nils visited the music room with the girls while Linnea took care of Billy on the sun deck. Nils had seen one of the two music rooms, when Lars gave him a brief tour of the ship. Each of the music rooms had a player piano with an extensive library of songs engraved onto rollers that would "play" the piano keys when the mechanism was wound up by a hand-crank.

Nils thought he would have some fun with girls and sat down at the player piano, gave the handle a few cranks and pretended to play on the keys when it began to play a "Rag Time" song—a current favorite with the "Charleston" dance craze.

Asta and Siri had seen their father play the piano many times before and were not the least suspicious that anything was awry. They had never seen a player piano before, however, so Nils cleverly justified the crank saying, "This was a self-tuning device for a very modern piano.”

Nils usually played by ear and easily followed the keys with his nimble fingers as the girls clapped their hands in rhythm to the light music. Suddenly, however, Nils stood up, walked away from the piano and also began to clap his hands in unison with the girls. Their eyes grew wide with amazement as the piano continued to play by itself. Nils grabbed their hands and began to dance with them, ignoring their expressions of disbelief as the piano played on.

“Papa!” they both said as one,
“that piano is playing all by itself! How does it do that?”

Nils continued to whirl them both about and without breaking stride or cracking a smile he explained, “Well how about that” as he looked back at the piano, “I’m not quite sure, but I think this must be one of those magical pianos. I’ve never seen one myself but they say they only play in front of magical people.”

Asta’s eyes widened even further as she completely bought the story her father was telling her. Siri, on the other hand, was not so easily convinced, as she was only too familiar with her father’s penchant for creating the most wonderful tall tales. He always told them with such a straight face, which invariably had the effect of giving more credence to the story. But this time she knew something was not quite right. "Come on Papa", she pleaded, "how does it really work?" Nils realized he couldn't continue with his ruse anymore and so he began to patiently reveal the secrets of a player piano. The three of them spent a good portion of the day selecting songs from the extensive library of music stored on the shelves. The girls would take turns placing the rollers in the piano and turning the crank. Each time the piano played another song they would have the same excited reaction of amazement. The novelty never seemed to wear off.

Meanwhile Asta was busy chasing Billy up and down the promenade deck…he never seemed to run out of energy. The sun shone brightly, intensified further by the reflection off the water, and both of them began to feel the heat of the afternoon. Linnea decided it would be a good idea to take off Billy's shirt for a while as he was beginning to perspire in the warm afternoon sun. At times Billy would accept holding hands with his mother as they walked on the main deck, but for the most part he was more in the mood to run. He managed to interrupt more than a few games of shuffleboard before he succumbed to the need for his daily afternoon nap. Only then did Linnea have a chance to relax on a deck chair with Billy curled up in her lap, fast asleep. The combination of the warm sun on her face and the soft breeze off the ocean were enough to cause Linnea to close her eyes and drift off. She was barely aware of the small talk of the passengers as they walked by.

After a good forty-five minute nap, Billy awoke with renewed energy, eager to explore the rest of the ship and terrorize all on board. For the time being, however, Linnea managed to grip his hand firmly and urge him to walk at her own pace. As they continued their walk, several of the lady passengers would stop them to smile and remark, "My, what a cute little boy you have there, although it looks like he's had a bit too much sun today. You really need to put some light cream on that." They wouldn't walk more than another fifteen feet when someone else would stop them again to give advice about sunburn. "I always found that towels with cold water helped take away the sting", or "A little light coating of milk will surely help him sleep tonight", or "I always found sour cream to take care of that", or "My mother used to put cold cream for removing makeup to sooth that burn." Linnea listened politely and thanked them for their advice but she already knew what to do; vinegar was the answer. It was a remedy she learned from Dr. Baker when Siri, at age four, had spent too much time in the sun on a picnic. It worked!

Later that afternoon, on her way back to their cabin, she managed to pass by the galley and convince one of the servers to let her have a small bottle of white vinegar. She had found Nils and the girls in the social hall as they were just leaving the music room. The girls excitedly greeted their mother and Billy, recounting all that they had seen and done with Nils including a tour of the reading room, the smoking room, the telegraph system, the telephones, and of course their favorite, the player piano. They were so intent on telling their mother about their adventures that they didn't even notice how red their little brother was.

They all headed back together to their quarters to clean up and change for dinner as they continued to talk about the wonderful time they were having so far. It wouldn't be long, however, before they encountered a small bump in the road to completing an almost perfect day.

Once in the room, Linnea had decided it might be a good idea to treat Billy's sunburn before it started to bother him during dinner. She carefully opened the bottle of vinegar, splashed some into the palm of her hand and approached Billy to apply some to his back. Little Billy immediately sensed this acrid smelling stuff was intended for him and while it was Nils's job to hold him steady, he didn't want to grip too tightly on Billy's sunburn sensitive arms. It proved to be a big mistake.

As Linnea moved forward, Billy jerked backward escaping Nils's grip, as he slammed hard into the dresser. This wouldn't have been such a disaster except for the fact that on top of the dresser was a jar of pickled herring that Linnea had brought from home as a special treat for Nils. The jolt to the dresser tipped over the jar of pickled herring and it rolled too quickly off the top for Nils to grab before it crashed loudly to the cabin floor. What a commotion! In the excitement, Linnea had spilled a good portion of the vinegar on herself, pickled herring was all over the floor mingled with broken glass and Billy was now crying uncontrollably. The smell in the room was overpowering as the girls covered their faces and opened the door for some relief. Nils quickly opened the porthole and turned on the small electric fan to help with the ventilation. Linnea followed the girls' lead as she took Billy by the hand and led him out into the hallway, while Nils remained behind and picked up the broken glass and herring.

Out in the hallway, the girls continued to whine about the foul smell as Linnea was trying her best to console Billy who was crying from the stinging sunburn, the bump on his head where he hit the dresser and life in general. It was enough of a ruckus to arouse the curiosity of the neighboring cabin and a well-dressed middle-aged woman opened her door to see what the disturbance was all about. Linnea was more than a little embarrassed about the unfortunate string of events and certainly was not prepared to answer the questions she knew this woman was about to ask.

It was too late as the woman now joined them in the hallway and innocently asked the obvious, "I couldn't help but hear the cries of a child and wondered if I might be of some..." She abruptly stopped in mid-sentence, "My goodness what is that awful smell?" she remarked, quickly withdrawing a handkerchief from her sleeve to cover her face.

Linnea, now totally embarrassed and not in the mood to explain the whole story, quickly said with a forced smile, "Well, the little one here, as you can see, had a bit too much sun today. While I was trying to apply some vinegar to soothe the sting, he jumped back and managed to spill most of it on me."

"Oh dear", the woman said, "how unfortunate, but you know besides the vinegar I could swear there is a distinct odor of fish".

Linnea quickly countered, not wanting to reveal that they had herring in the room, "Oh that's probably the smell of cod liver oil. We always give a daily dose to the children. Keeps them in good health you know" she added for emphasis.

The woman nodded in agreement and was almost ready to believe Linnea's explanation when Nils walked out of the cabin with a washbowl full of pickled herring and a wide smile on his face. There must have been two dozen of the oily fish piled high in their cabin's porcelain bowl which was normally used for washing their hands and face. He gave a quick glance to the woman and courteously said, "Good afternoon!" Then, without hesitation he turned to Linnea announcing proudly, "I'm just going to take these to the bathroom and wash them off", he said with sense of purpose, "They are still perfectly good and we certainly don't want to waste a treat like this now do we?"

There wasn't much Linnea could say or do. Nonetheless, she feebly tried to explain, "Well, you know my husband and I are from Sweden and fish is a favorite..." But it was too late, and Linnea found herself talking to the woman's backside, as she quickly re-entered her cabin. The woman closed the door with just enough force to let Linnea know that she didn't need any further explanations.

Linnea was once again alone in the hallway smelling of vinegar and fish. It was not, however, in her nature to let something like this upset her. She could always find the light-hearted side of things as she turned to the girls with a big smile and said, "Apparently she didn't like the way we smelled. Well I didn't exactly like the smell of her cheap perfume either." Holding her nose and sticking out her tongue, she said "Ufta!" for emphasis. It was enough to break the tension and make the girls giggle. Little Billy didn't understand what was said, but intuitively sensed some fun and stopped crying momentarily.

Linnea could hardly fault Nils, for he was only doing what was natural for a man that grew up in a family of twelve. Food was a precious commodity and not to be wasted. Today we make a joke of the "five second" rule, however, for Nils it was irrelevant whether it was five seconds, five minutes or five hours; food was not to be wasted.

Outside of a few cold stares from their cabin neighbor who witnessed the "The Great Herring Incident", the remainder of their trip to Savannah continued to be a relaxing and rejuvenating experience for the entire family. Nils knew they were only into their third day away from Boston and it was much too soon to realize any change in Linnea's condition, but he couldn't help but believe there was a perceptible improvement. It may have been a bit of wishful thinking, but to Nils it was undeniable that the easy smile, mischievous sense of humor and confident demeanor that was always the center of his love for her, was beginning to return. Even more apparent, however, was the physical transformation that was taking place as the sun had already added much needed color to her face and there was a noticeably higher level of energy in her step. Linnea was a free spirit and the atmosphere aboard the ship out in the open sea coupled with the sense of adventure for their new life in

Florida seemed to have renewed her zest for life; a quality that Nils had always found so attractive. Even though his daily log, kept for Dr. Baker, showed a continued reminder of her disease with occasional higher than normal temperatures, Nils was encouraged with her early progress. They were at sea for almost three days when they approached the mouth of the Savannah River, at which point they headed up river to the port. Forced to reduce speed to five knots, it would take them another two hours before they docked in Savannah. As they approached land for the first time in nearly three days, Nils, Linnea and family joined the other passengers on deck.

First in their sight was one of the barrier islands as the ship took aim between the northern side of Tybee Island and the South Carolina/Georgia border of the Savannah River. Tybee Island had become a popular vacation spot, especially for those living in Savannah, desperate to escape the heat and humidity of the summer. Vacation homes were set back behind the dunes and beach facing the Atlantic Ocean. They were built on stilts with large wrap-around porches to take full advantage of the ocean breeze. A small permanent community of a few thousand would swell to ten-fold during the summer months when the rich and famous rented houses on the beachfront. It was a daily spectacle when they would parade along the wooden pier and beaches. The men dressed formally in coats, ties and hats, while the women, equally overdressed by today's standards, sported long dresses, high heels, broad brimmed hats and twirling parasols.

Nils was quick to point out to the children one of the last lighthouses they would see when they passed the Tybee Lighthouse located on the northern tip of the island. As they sailed by the lighthouse they could see parts of Fort Screven slowly coming into view. The heavily armed fort was built in the late 1890's to protect the Port of Savannah, joining other such military installations along the eastern seaboard designed to protect the U.S. Atlantic Coast from foreign intruders. Originally hidden by sand dunes and the seas tall oat grass, the thick walls of the fort were now partially exposed due to the construction of a new highway joining the island and the city of Savannah.

As their ship continued up river, the family was treated to a variety of wildlife that they had never seen before. The children had already experienced the excitement of dolphins that crisscrossed along the bow of the ship as it had slowed to make its original turn into the mouth of the Savannah River. Now passing the end of Tybee Island the ship began to slowly weave its way through the interior islands of Cockspur, Elba and Hutchinson. Each of these islands offered up something new—sandpipers running along the narrow dark beaches, gull-billed terns feeding in the shallow marshland waters and brown pelicans gliding in tight formation. Nils smiled to himself and was delighted to see the joy on the children's faces as the watched the ongoing spectacle…it was quite a show. He felt surer than ever that they had made the right decision.

THIRTEEN

Culture Shock

At long last the *City of Columbus* arrived at the port of Savannah. Nils and family were on deck watching their ship being pulled and pushed into the dock by several hard working tugboats. The docking space was large enough to accommodate four of The Savannah Lines' ships. The Savannah Line owned more than one mile of water front property. It was considered one of the finest in America with regard to expediting the transfer of both cargo and passengers from ship to train. There were huge wharves on either side of the docks where stored goods (mostly cotton) could be loaded onto railroad tracks.

The docking process took a good half-hour, which allowed Nils to view much of the port from his vantage point on the hurricane deck. Peering down, he saw row after row of barrels filled with provisions for the US Navy that were to be transported north. Mule teams strained to pull carts laden with cotton bales along the docks, which were loaded mostly by hand truck through the ship's side ports. The sight of so much cotton was impressive, but it was a mere fraction of the amount that the port handled in years past. The cotton trade, which helped build the Port of Savannah into a US leader in marine transport, was going through a transition. The infestation of cotton by the boll weevil had destroyed almost the entire Georgia crop and a good portion of the remaining cotton producing states. Also, Massachusetts' textile industries were beginning to relocate to the south to be closer to the source of raw materials. As a result, the cargo traffic through the Port of Savannah throughout the early 1920's was slowing down.

Nils was captivated by the predominance of black workers. He had never before seen so many black people congregated in one place. They seemed to be everywhere. He watched them push handcarts loaded with bales of cotton and barrels of Navy cargo up the ramps and into the holds of the ships. Living in Boston, Nils was never exposed to more than the occasional black person. The black population in Boston at the time was only a bit over two percent while by contrast that of Savannah hovered closer to fifty. The Irish had managed to dominate and fill most of the jobs at the low end of the pay scale. Despite the general migration of blacks to the North after the cotton crops succumbed to the boll weevil, Savannah still had a large black population.

Their train would not be leaving for several more hours so Nils decided it would be a good idea to have some lunch at the station while they were waiting to have luggage transferred from the ship to the train. There was an informal little restaurant located inside the Central of Georgia train station where the family sat down to eat. They had barely sat down when a woman, dressed in a white uniform with a matching white hat pinned to her blond hair, greeted them.

She seemed friendly, but the only word Nils understood was 'lunch'. Uncertain that he understood her, he responded with a tentative, "Yes please, may we have some menus?"

"No need for menus, I got it all right up here", as she pointed to her head. She proceeded to rattle off the lunch specials while everyone, especially Nils, strained to understand what she was saying.

Was this really English? Nils thought to himself.

Fortunately, she had assigned numbers to each special, giving Nils a means to respond.

"We will have two of number one and three of number four please" Nils said with a smile.

"All righty then", she said. "Will ya'll be wantin some grits with lunch? There's no extra charge."

She was faced with five blank incredulous faces at the table.

"Did you say grits?" Nils finally asked. "What exactly are grits?"

"Oh my", she said with a smile. "I kinda guessed ya'll ain't from around here, but you just can't leave without trying some grits. Hard to explain exactly what they're like so I'll just bring out a bowl and ya'll can share." And with that she disappeared into the kitchen.

Nils and the children had a little chuckle over the waitress's strange accent; Linnea, however, was not amused. Out of ear shot of the children, she leaned over to Nils, "I may not have understood much of what she said, but I certainly do remember her calling you "sweetie or hon or honey" at list six or seven times and it didn't look like you objected at all!"

"Now Linnea, don't overreact, that's probably just a custom peculiar to this part of the country. Besides it's only natural that she makes a pass at such a good looking man such as myself" he said, trying to make light of the situation.

Because of the "language barrier" Nils had only guessed at what to order, but when the food finally arrived they were all pleasantly surprised. There were generous portions of biscuits and gravy, mashed potatoes, stewed peas and carrots served with a mountain of crispy fried chicken. Even the grits were devoured as the waitress showed them how to liven them up with salt, pepper and plenty of butter. It was all washed down with something called "Lemonade" which was another new treat for the whole family, especially the children. It was all so very good that even little Billy managed to sit still through the entire meal.

Mary Joe reappeared, amazed, but at the same time pleased by all the empty plates. "My, you folks sure can pack it away. Especially you sweetie", directing her gaze at Linnea. "Honey, I sure wish I could eat like that and keep your girlish figure."

Linnea by now was feeling a little embarrassed, not so much by what Mary Joe said, but rather how she said it. She could feel the "I told you so" look from Nils as she began to realize that the "honey, hon and sweetie" remarks were merely a matter of local custom.

They all refused the offers of dessert, which included something called Pecan Pie. That and the peach cobbler looked very tempting but no one had room for another ounce of food. After Nils settled the bill and they were about to leave, Mary Joe came up with a question that really tickled Linnea and Nils.

"You have to excuse me, but ya'll have the strangest accent and I was wondering where you was from?" she asked with an apologetic but straight face.

"We are from Sweden", Nils responded with a smile trying not to chuckle. *Talk about the pot calling the kettle black,* he thought.

"Oh my", said a baffled Mary Joe, "never heard of that place before. Well anyhow, nice to meet ya. Have a good trip and ya'll come back real soon."

Out on the street, Nils began to feel the rising heat and humidity of the Savannah afternoon. The cool breeze on board the ship had camouflaged the oppressive heat that was now becoming trapped between the buildings of the city…the thick moist air felt like a heavy blanket. Nils's shirt was already soaked with perspiration and he looked at Linnea with concern. He hoped that this new climate hadn't already compromised her lungs. Linnea sensed his concern and quickly gave a reassuring smile while returning to the business at hand…keeping an eye on the children. Nils then made a feeble attempt at a Southern accent as he addressed the family.

"Now ya'll better make a stop at the bathrooms before ya'll board the train." The girls giggled a bit, Billy paid little attention to what was said and Linnea just shook her head with mild disapproval.

Standing in front of the bathrooms, Nils was astonished to see that there were more than the usual choices. Signs clearly stated in bold letters "WHITE ONLY". He had noticed similar signs before entering the café and for the first time began to feel, not only read about, the brutal reality of the word…segregation.

Now that the girls could read, he realized it would only be a matter of time before they would be asking questions. They would be living in a southern state and inevitably they would be confronted with a strong local opinion on the difference between whites and blacks.

Just then, little Siri exited the bathroom with a direct question for her father. "What does 'white only' mean?" Nils was quick to delay the inevitable discussion for the time being and said, "We'll talk about it when we get settled on the train. Let's hurry along now."

But his reprieve was all too brief. When they approached the train, another distorted view of the Negro's place in southern society quickly came in to view. The well-dressed "aristocracy" of Savannah was milling about the train station's platform and, next to their mountains of baggage, uniformed Negro porters were answering their every beck and call.

"George, can you help me with this please?" a smartly dressed southern gentleman shouted in the direction of a nearby porter. At first Nils thought it was an extremely polite gesture to recognize the porter by his first name…until he heard someone else say to another porter, "Oh George, over here please as soon as you can." It wasn't long before Nils realized that all of the porters responded to the generic name of "George". It wasn't a form of friendly endearment at all, but rather a cruel disregard for their existence as individuals. They were viewed as little more than a service provided by the railway system to be exploited by the ticket-bearing patrons. Many of the porters were reduced to performing impromptu dance steps and tricks at the request of the all-white crowd boarding the train. The porters complied in hopes of receiving a small tip, which was sometimes forthcoming and often times not.

The Pullman Company, the founder of the sleeping car, was the largest employer of black males in the country during the 1920's. Porters generally made more money than the average black man; however, the hours and shifts were extremely long, stretching over several weeks without a day off. Most worked close to four hundred hours per month performing a wide range of never-ending duties including handling baggage, shining shoes, providing passenger security and dusting ashes from the railings and clothes of the passengers. The porter, of course, was also expected to answer the call of passengers for whatever reason and at whatever hour. The more important job of the Pullman porter, however, was to prepare the car for sleeping during the evening and then remove the heavy curtains and bedding to convert them into seating in the morning.

True to the southern "tradition" of the time, blacks were not allowed in the sleeping cars and were relegated to a separate passenger car at the end of the train.

Now that they were on board, Nils was determined to talk with the girls as soon as the train was under way and the excitement of their first train trip had begun to subside. Suddenly, the train jolted forward from the mighty pull of the steam engine and, as the train left the station, the girls were still in high anticipation of new sites to come.

Trains were quite comfortable in the early twenties as they had been the only form of long distance travel in the United States for several decades. The automobile had only been around for a few years, plane travel was non-existent and steamships obviously could not penetrate the interior of the country. Trains, on the other hand, had been evolving over the past seventy-five years and were not only well equipped and luxurious, but very fast. Typically at sixty to seventy miles per hour, passenger trains traveled unimpeded by traffic of any kind over well-maintained rails. Cushioned by a good suspension system, their top speeds exceeded 100 miles per hour. There were comfortable padded seats, large dining cars, smoking cars as well as sleeping cars for a good night's rest; all while the train proceeded non-stop towards its destination.

Their next stop was Jacksonville, Florida. It had become the busiest train station in the country as rail travel reached its peak in the early 20's. This increase in rail traffic was due mainly to the huge popularity of Florida as both a vacation spot and prime area for purchasing real estate. The one hundred and forty mile trip from Savannah to Jacksonville only had a few brief stops in between and would not take more than a few hours. After the first hour, the girls began to tire of the repetitive scenery, and slowly they peeled themselves away from the window. Billy was now fast asleep, taking a late afternoon nap cradled in his mother's arms.

Dressed in a crisp white uniform, one of the porters passed by carrying a silver thermos filled with ice water for anyone who asked. The sight of him prompted Siri to return to her question of the "white only" signs she had seen. Intuitively, she had begun to put things together and thought she might know the answer to her own question, but wanted confirmation from her father, as she asked, "Papa you said you would explain about the signs on the bathrooms."

This isn't going to be easy, Nils thought to himself. He

had worked this out in his own mind over the years but knew it would be a struggle to explain such a weighty subject to a nine year old.

He had come to the realization that prejudice was simply based on a person's perception of a difference. The difference could be a person's color, speech pattern, height, the way they walked or how they dressed; it really didn't matter. Nils rationalized that in order for someone to recognize a difference they must believe that some sort of standard existed for each of these conditions. Those who were prejudiced honestly believed that what they saw in a black person or heard from someone's accent was a deviation from some standard.

But, he thought, *what if there really weren't a standard? If one were to imagine any standard to be a non-descript wooden pole around which everyone revolved there would be no dissimilarity. Without a standard by which to judge, there would be no reason for prejudice. People simply are who they are, no more and no less.*

Nils reached for the journal Dr. Baker had given him to record the progress of Linnea's condition, and sat down between Asta and her older sister Siri. He had remembered that as a young boy, it was much easier to learn a new concept if you could somehow draw it. Segregation was a topic much too difficult to explain with only words, so with pen in hand, he drew a large circle with a dot in the center on an empty page of the journal.

Although the Vensberg family did not practice their religion with as much rigidity as was custom while they lived in Sweden, they did attend the Lutheran Church every Sunday and made certain that the children were well schooled in their religious beliefs. Drawing on this experience seemed to be the easiest means to drive home his point.

"Now, think of all the people in the world, from every country and of every skin color", he began, "lined up shoulder to shoulder on the edge of this circle. Then imagine the dot in the center of this circle", he continued, "as representing God." While tracing the circle again with his pen for emphasis, he explained, "What this means is that everyone on the edge of the circle; white, black, short, tall, including you and I, are no closer or farther away from God who is at the center." For emphasis he drew several lines radiating out from the center to the circle's edge.

"This is how it is supposed to be. However, some people like those in this area of the country—at least most of the white people—mistakenly believe that they should be in the center of the circle with more privileges. While we are in Florida you are going to see that black people are not allowed in most restaurants, they are required to attend separate schools, use separate bathrooms and drinking fountains. The white people will try to convince you that this is the way it should be. Whenever that happens, just remember this circle and who is in the center and you will always have the right answer."

The explanation seemed to satisfy Siri for the moment, although Nils knew it would not be the last he heard of the subject; the innocence and relentless curiosity of Siri would not allow it to end there. Fortunately, for the moment, all their attention returned to the view of the new countryside streaming by the windows of the train.

The Jacksonville station was undergoing massive expansion to accommodate the growth of tourism. Jacksonville was now considered the gateway to Florida, the fruition of an idea of two wealthy entrepreneurs…both named Henry. Years before the Florida land boom, Henry Flagler and Henry Plant began to independently consolidate all of the smaller railways into their individual railway systems. Although the two Henrys steered their enterprises in different geographical directions, their business plans were quite similar. Henry Flagler concentrated on hugging the eastern seaboard of Florida, beginning in Jacksonville and eventually extending his railroad through Miami to the Florida Keys.

Henry Plant also began in Jacksonville but chose to expand towards the west of Florida into Tampa. Both of these railroad giants would strategically build hotels in the principal cities along their routes to both accommodate existing tourists and attract future business.

Henry Plant's crowning jewel was the Tampa Bay Hotel, which was one of the most exclusive and expensive hotels in America at the time. Built in 1891, the hotel had more than five hundred rooms, most of which were lavishly decorated and included bathrooms, electric fans and telephones—all of where were firsts for the hotel industry. A spur from his train system brought guests directly to the hotel where they could disembark straight into the hotel lobby. It was one of the first hotels to charge an unheard of $100 per night. Entertainment included wild game hunting, deep-sea fishing, sailing and golf. The hotel even had its own racetrack.

Linnea and Nils, although traveling on one of Henry Plant's trains, were heading towards a far more modest destination and life style. Now only a few hours away from Tampa, Nils was aware of his increasing anxiety, as they got closer to their final stop. He had been relatively at ease and confident a few days ago when they left Boston, but as they sailed to Savannah his apprehension seemed to grow with each passing mile. The novelty of the train's almost triumphant arrival in the very center of each town began to wear off and was replaced with worrisome thoughts of caring for his family in a place that was completely foreign to him and without certainty of employment.

One of Many Entrances to Tampa Bay Hotel.
Courtesy, Tampa-Hillsborough County Pubic Library System.

As the train was now only a few hours from DeSoto Park, Nils sensed that they both were feeling anxious and he asked Siri to watch over her sister and little brother Billy so he could talk to Linnea for a while. It was an opportunity to calm her unease and reassure her that they were doing the right thing.

Holding her hand he offered, "Just a few hours now and we'll be there. How are you feeling?"

"To be honest, I am really nervous now that I know we are almost there," she admitted. "I know you are doing this for me, but dragging the kids all this way, leaving your job and friends behind…it seems like such a great risk to take."

"If it's any comfort", he told her, squeezing her hand for emphasis, "I feel the same way, but we have made our decision together and we will make the best of it. You have to believe in your heart that it is the right thing to do or it will disrupt our chances for success."

She knew he was right and took comfort in the fact that she was not alone with this troubled feeling about their future.

FOURTEEN

The Tin-Canners

Desoto Park, for the most part, was exactly the way they had imagined it to be. The large tent they were provided with was in a heavily wooded area that gave shade from the sun during the day and some cover from the heavy summer rains. They were surrounded by other "Tin-Canners" who had come from as far away as Minnesota and Wisconsin...people who had traveled hundreds of miles in their cars to either vacation in the sun, purchase some land for investment or both. The atmosphere was one of levity and good fun, as most of these travelers were taking some well-deserved time off work and were prepared to enjoy the Florida sun. There was an almost carnival-like atmosphere. Everyone was relaxed and relieved to be away from the tensions of work. Pony rides, impromptu horseshoe tournaments and music from guitars, banjo's—even

Nils's violin— put everyone in a festive mood. Nils and Linnea found it to be a comfortable place…one where friends were easily made.

Little Billy and the girls loved to wander off into neighboring tents where they were met by little resistance from the occupants who were enjoying their vacation. One neighboring tent dweller seemed to have a particular fondness for Billy. He would frequently bring him back to the Vensberg tent just to reassure Linnea that the little boy was all right and not to worry. The man's name was Otto Bendler. He had come down to Florida from Harvey, Illinois with his son. It was their second trip to Florida and Otto was looking to invest in some land purely for speculative reasons. There was no shortage of deals to be made and many of them involved little money down with the idea that the value would rapidly increase.

Otto had just purchased a small tract of land on the outskirts of DeSoto Park. This deal was initiated through one of the many "Binder Boys"—men who were hired to take deposits for realtors who did not want to sit and wait in the hot sun for clients to visit properties that were in remote locations. These young men, who were often college students, would baby-sit these properties and take deposit checks (usually ten percent) as a binder towards the purchase of property administered by a real estate agent. Their commission was made as soon as the check cleared the bank. The Florida land boom was so extensive that this was the only way the real estate industry could service the enormous surge in speculative buyers.

"Tin Canners" relaxing in DeSoto Park.
Courtesy, Tampa-Hillsborough County Public Library System

Nils and Otto became fast friends while spending evenings outside their neighboring tents talking about what had brought them to Florida. Otto had taken over his father's small construction company in Harvey, Illinois after his dad collapsed from a near fatal heart attack.

Now, he was a struggling contractor in the local housing industry; he had managed to build his business into a fairly substantial company that included construction of commercial buildings. He also assisted city planners in the design of new roads to accommodate the rapidly expanding automobile industry. His son had joined him in the enterprise two years ago and they were now at the point where they could afford to take a few weeks off to both relax and invest some of their hard earned money in the Florida real estate market.

L to R: Otto's Son, Siri Vensberg, and Otto Bendler

After hearing Nils's story, Otto was very interested in his experience as a carpenter and cabinetmaker. He promised Nils that, just as soon as Linnea had recovered enough from her illness, there would be a job waiting for him in Harvey—provided he could find the means to make the trip up north. When Linnea heard about that, she was especially interested. That move, would take her closer to her brother Victor who had a successful farm in Piper City, Illinois. She knew it may be only a remote possibility with so many uncertainties in their lives right now, but it provided a glimmer of hope and a further incentive to make the best of their current situation. Life was becoming more tenuous with each passing day.

They had only been there a few days now, but Nils quickly came to the realization that his ambitions for Florida and his family would not be easily fulfilled. Although the campsite provided for their every need and then some, the cost of these services was far beyond their means. The expenditure of staying a few weeks in DeSoto Park for most of the "tin-canners" was easily affordable. They were on vacation…a treat for a short stay in the sun. Nils's situation, however, was completely different. He needed to find employment quickly or he would be forced to look elsewhere for a more affordable place to live in Florida. His efforts to find anything to meet his family's needs had proven unproductive so far. The only immediate source of income, though meager, was picking oranges alongside the migrant workers that harvested the fruit each year.

The quandary of what to do was the principal topic of their evening chats, which lasted well past the colorful Florida sunsets and into the night. They both felt they had to act soon as any extension of their stay in DeSoto Park would quickly drain their small amount of savings.

Men on Ladders Picking Oranges: Tampa Fla.
Courtesy, Tampa-Hillsborough County Public Library System

Finally, a plan emerged between Otto and Nils. Nils and his family would stay on Otto's newly acquired property on the outskirts of Tampa. It would give Otto the means to look after his investment and, at the same time, provide Nils with a rent-free place to live. He offered to buy the family a tent from the manager of the park and would help move them to the property before he returned to the Chicago area. It was the best Nils could hope for under the circumstances.

And so towards the end of his stay at DeSoto Park, Otto began to help Nils and Linnea pack their few belongings into his car along with the ten by fifteen foot tent purchased from the park director. The land that Otto had purchased was about fifteen miles from the campsite. It would require two trips, as there wasn't enough room in his Model T to fit everyone. This was the first time that the children would ride in a car and the adventure was one of total amazement. Otto was greeted with applause and giggles from them as he cranked up the engine, put the car in gear, and finally honked the horn several times while the car lurched forward.

They chose a site for their new "home" under the shade of several cypress trees near the only fresh water well on the land. At first, like all things new, it was exciting for everyone to help set up the tent in their new surroundings—but the feeling quickly diminished the day Otto and his son left for their return trip to Chicago. The harsh reality for Nils and Linnea was that they were now more alone than ever, removed from the security of friends, family and most of all, the creature comforts that they had taken for granted. But they quickly adapted, made the best of their circumstances, and never lost focus on their principal goal, which was to return Linnea to good health.

Every evening Nils would alternate hoisting Siri and Asta on his shoulders to reach up and gather fresh moss from the cypress trees. The moss was used to stuff pillowcases and sheets and provided some comfort on the stiff cots they all slept on. Cleanliness was always a priority for Linnea. She insisted that the moss be removed the next morning and a fresh batch harvested every evening before retiring to bed. The routine was not a chore for the girls as they enjoyed being with their father and they felt that they were contributing to the family's comfort. It was the same for the rest of their chores, which included pumping water from the well, filling up the buckets and carrying them to their mother for cooking, drinking, washing clothes and dishes. Little Billy loved to tag along with the girls and occasionally dip his head under the water stream of the pump to cool off from the oppressive Florida summer heat. Nils on the other hand would struggle to provide for the family over the next several months. Outside of the odd carpentry job he found at DeSoto Park, picking fruit remained his only option to make ends meet.

He could tolerate the hard work, but what upset him the most was the toll it was taking on his hands. The cuts from picking fruit made it difficult, if not impossible at times, to play his violin, which had always been a great release for him. But Nils would never complain or show his disappointment. He was grateful to make the sacrifice as long as Linnea's health showed steady signs of improvement.

Fortunately, the sun and fresh air continued to work its magic and the frequency of her coughing diminished with each passing week. Her rich dark brown tan intensified her bright blue eyes and gave her the picture of perfect health. It was an amazing transformation and gave Nils the motivation to carry on.

Their economic situation took a turn for the better when Nils found work with a new company called "QuickBilt". Based in South Carolina, the A.C. Tuxbury Lumber Co. had come up with an opportunistic idea that was designed to take advantage of the Florida land boom. Tuxbury came up with a solution—a train to Tampa that could carry the necessary materials for erecting a house in only a few days. Nils was hired as part of the crew who would build houses with these pre-constructed pieces on land purchased by the "tin-canners." Now, they could watch their new bungalows built within the timeframe of their brief stay in Florida before they returned to their homes up north. The money Nils earned from "QuickBilt" was not much, but it was a steady income and gave him the pleasure of doing the type of work he was trained to do.

QuickBilt Bungalow
Courtesy, Tampa-Hillsborough County Public Library System

He was not only a tireless worker but there was a special gift Nils had that allowed him to accomplish almost twice what other men could do in a day. Nils was ambidextrous. When most men would tire from hammering or sawing, Nils could simply switch hands with equal efficiency and continue on working. Nils, a natural "lefty", was forced to use only his right hand while growing up in Sweden, as it was considered improper and something of a handicap to be left-handed. There were no such restrictions in America and it proved to be a valuable asset in his line of work. It was certainly a trait that did not go unnoticed by Otto.

Nils's work at QuickBilt gave him the initiative to build the very first home for his family. It would be the first of four homes that he would design and build by himself. This first one was a simple log cabin made from the surrounding trees felled on Otto Bender's property and it was built three feet off the ground—mostly to discourage animal intruders. Living in the tent was a fun adventure for the family but Linnea had grown tired of the occasional four-legged visitor and was more than a bit concerned about snakes. Four steps led to the only door that accessed the cabin. Inside, the cabin was divided into three rooms; one bedroom for Linnea and Nils and another for the children, where simple bunk beds were built into one corner for the girls and another wooden frame bed on the opposite wall for Billy. The third room served as kitchen, living and dining room. There was only one small window on the front wall next to the door, which afforded a limited view of the outside and some light during the day. The girls with a bucket of soapy water and some stiff brushes scrubbed the pine floor religiously every Saturday. Aesthetically, it was not much to look at but was a great improvement from the tent.

More importantly, it was a place that gave the family a sense of permanence and stability.

In June of 1920, Otto Bender and his son returned to Florida to check on their land investment and pay the Vensberg family a visit. Otto was pleasantly surprised to see the fine job Nils had done with the small cabin. He was equally pleased with the improved health of Linnea and hoped that they both would now feel confident that it had improved enough to accept his offer to move north. His Chicago business was growing and he could use the talents of Nils during this period of expansion.

Nils, on the other hand, had sent his well-kept journal of Linnea's health back to Dr. Baker in Boston and was waiting for his reply. He had anticipated Otto's return and was prepared to accept the job offer in Chicago but wanted to have the final approval of his good friend Dr. Baker.

Dr. Baker was quick to write back. After reviewing Nils's journal, he felt that it was safe for Linnea to leave Florida and travel to Chicago but he was quick to point out that he had some concerns over their move to a cold climate. Relieved that they would be living away from the congestion of the city proper, he added that ultimately it would be Nils who would have to make the final decision. Dr. Baker trusted that he would make the right one.

Linnea with her three children before
leaving Florida for Chicago

Nils and Linnea had discussed the move over the past several months and although they knew they could not remain in Florida much longer, they wanted to assure themselves that they were not leaving prematurely because of the pressure to find a more stable environment for the children. The girls had to walk three miles to school and the isolation of living so far away from the nearest town and friends was becoming a burden. The excitement and adventure of living in the wilderness had long since worn thin and they both felt it was time to return the family to a place where the children could thrive in an environment that had a community of families, business, and schools.

Otto was extremely pleased when Nils told him he was ready to accept the offer and make the move to Chicago. He told Nils that he would pay him for the cabin that he built on the property so that he would have some extra money to make the trip. Otto was eager to have a place for himself and his son to stay when they visited Florida. It would save them the money they would normally have to pay at DeSoto Park. He even went so far as to suggest to Nils that he buy a used Model T and make the drive back to Chicago with him. Although Linnea's eyes lit up at the mere thought of traveling by car, Nils was quick to dash any hope of such an adventure.

Too often, he had seen Otto struggle to change tires during his short stay in Florida. The roads in 1920 were little more than two deep ruts and when it rained, the mud made it almost impossible to make any headway. The model T's windshield and canvas top were the only protection from the rain. There were no side windows, only some pulled down shades or flaps of cloth that let in more water than they would keep out. Nils had nightmarish visions of what it would be like for three small children cramped in an unreliable car for some nineteen hundred miles—a trip that could take several days.

"Thanks for the offer Otto", Nils said, "but I would much prefer to take the train. Maybe someday after we settle down in Chicago we can think about getting ourselves a car. Now, however, is not the time."

Nils, who was from a culture that stressed punctuality, was much more comfortable with the relative reliability of the American rail system. They decided that they would write to Linnea's brother, Victor, and hoped to visit him on the way to Chicago. Nils wanted to be certain they arrived on the specific date that they had set. He felt that it would be inconsiderate to make Victor's family wait for them based on the unpredictable timetable of a trip by automobile. The decision not to go by automobile was somewhat disappointing for Linnea but in the end she knew Nils was doing the right thing.

As usual, Nils's intuition proved to be correct. It would have been a long and very uncomfortable trip to Chicago via automobile, especially with three small children. Most of the roads in the early 20's were either not clearly marked or not named at all. It wasn't until 1925 that the government began to implement a unified system for identifying roads and it was much later that they developed a highway system. The roads tended to follow old wagon trails or sometimes the native Indian paths, which were not always the shortest routes between major cities. The better roads were not paved by asphalt or cement but merely sprayed with oil to help prevent erosion and give some semblance of rigidity. These oiled roads were only twenty percent of all roads in existence, so for the most part travelers had to contend with rutted wagon tracks that became impassable when it rained.

FIFTEEN

Next Stop Chicago

With the money Otto had given them for the cabin, Nils purchased train tickets for the family that would take them north through the Florida panhandle and then west to New Orleans. It was in New Orleans that they would board the Illinois Central's *Panama Line,* which made a regular seventeen-hour run to Chicago. It would allow them to make a stop in Effram Illlinois, some forty miles north of Champaign, where they could transfer to another train for the twenty-mile trip west to Piper City.

The route from Tampa to New Orleans by train was long and complicated, as there was no single railroad company that would take them directly to New Orleans. The many stops and transfers from different railroad lines left the family exhausted and irritable by the time they arrived in New Orleans.

Fortunately, the Illinois Central's *Panama Line* was an all-Pullman car with a straight and direct route to Chicago. Once the Pullman car was converted to sleeping accommodations, they could lie down in relative comfort.

Linnea would check on the children occasionally and would often find the girls with their faces pressed against the window to get a glimpse of the new countryside. Looking at the two sisters, Linnea smiled as she remembered the train trip from Hull to Liverpool that she had taken with her sister Frida.

The girls eventually tired of the limited view from their window and the regular almost hypnotic sound of the steel wheels clicking on the railroad tracks put them to sleep quickly. Nils and Linnea, on the other hand, could not sleep. It had been two years since they had left Boston and they missed the daily contact of family and friends. The time spent in Florida had been important for Linnea's return to good health, but it had also isolated them from the life they knew in Boston. They both were now eager to be reunited with their immediate family and looked forward to conversing in Swedish.

They slept for only a few fitful hours that night and at 5:30 A.M. they were excited to wake the children and get them ready for their stop at Effram Illinois. From there they would take another train twenty miles west to Piper City, where her brother would be waiting for them.

It was a tearful and joyous reunion when they finally met Victor at the Piper City train station. It had been nearly fifteen years since Linnea had last seen her brother and it was something of an adjustment for her. Victor seemed to have aged much more than the fifteen years they had been apart. His letters to her over the years had conveyed how hard he had to work to establish himself in this farm community, but the words he had written didn't prepare her for what she saw. It had taken a physical toll on his body. Victor was thinner than she remembered and his face was weathered from the years of exposure to the hot Illinois summers and the harsh brutal winters. But her concern was over-ridden by the warmth she felt in being once again with her family.

After they piled all their belonging into the horse drawn wagon that Victor had driven down to the station, they headed back to his farm. The trip was more than ten miles, but time flew as they tried to fill in the gaps of several years of separation. Plus the children were enjoying the ride in the back of the wagon and were wide-eyed at the endless rows of corn that seemed to stretch forever in any given direction.

As the wagon made its way up the last hundred yards of the well-rutted dirt road, the farmhouse and a large barn finally came into view. They were greeted by the barking of two large dogs that were excited to see a wagon full of guests. Much to the delight of the girls, dozens of chickens scurried about while the intermittent "mooing" of cows could be heard coming from the barn. They had read about the workings of a farm and the animals in school, but to actually see them up close and experience the sounds and even the smells was very exciting. When the wagon come to a stop in front of the farm house, the girls jumped off, lifted Billy down off the wagon, grabbed his hand and started to run after the chickens. Linnea thought about telling them to come back but after seeing how excited they were, she decided to let them go. Nils managed a half-hearted yell of "Be careful girls!!" but also realized that they needed to burn off some steam. It had been a long trip.

Victor's wife Emma and their nine year-old daughter, Bernice, were waiting on the front porch to greet Linnea and Nils. The four adults began to unload the wagon and carry the luggage up the front steps and onto a porch that wrapped around two sides of the house. A large calico cat on one of the white wooden rockers by the front door napped and seemed unperturbed by their noisy chatter and the shuffle of luggage.

When they entered the house, the smell of freshly baked bread coming from the kitchen greeted them. It was a comforting reminder to Nils and Linnea of the days spent in Boston. When the girls and Billy tired of chasing chickens, they joined the group in the front living room of the house. Introductions were made and Bernice took the children to her room at the back of the house.

Meanwhile, the four adults relaxed in the living room with a cup of coffee and began to catch up on the years that had gone by since Linnea last saw her brother Victor. For the most part, they had communicated regularly by mail ever since Linnea's arrival in Boston in 1910…there was very little between them that they did not already know. Victor, however, had been anxious to see Linnea in person, as he was especially concerned to see what toll her bout with tuberculosis had taken on her physical well-being. As Linnea discussed her illness with her brother, Victor was pleasantly surprised at how well she looked. There was no visible evidence that the disease had done any harm. Linnea was back to her normal weight and the Florida sun had done its magic giving her a deep tan that made her blue eyes sparkle.

Nils and Victor got along famously as if they had known each other for years. They shared similar stories of adapting to the American culture as they learned English and carved out a good life through hard work. They both agreed that the move to America had been the right decision and, unlike the Sweden they left behind, here at least, their efforts had been rewarded with some measure of success.

Linnea was excited to hear about Victor's early years in America. She was only fourteen when he left and had to rely on what her parents told her about Victor's circumstances. They did not always share all of what was in his letters home and she was fascinated to hear, first-hand, Victor's accounts of his experience in this new land.

A sponsor was required before anyone could immigrate to the United States to ensure that they would have a place to stay and would not be a burden on the government. Victor told them his sponsor, Sven Jurgensen, was a family friend of the Perssons in Malmo, Sweden. He had come to America in 1895 and was from a long line of family farmers. He had managed to eke out a living in Piper City, first as a farm hand and later as a landowner, by means of an inheritance from his former employer.

The farm that Sven had inherited was a combination of a run-down dairy farm and another large parcel of a hundred acres that was dedicated to row crops. Since Victor's farming expertise leaned more heavily towards dairy farming, Sven entrusted him to help in developing that end of the business. It was a perfect match—Sven's farming interest and experience was in corn and other row crop products. The dairy portion of the farm had been neglected for quite some time and it took Victor the better part of three years to bring it back to a profitable venture. Sven was pleased with Victor's work, especially since he had little interest in the dairy sector of the farm. Over time, through a profit sharing arrangement, he offered Victor the option to buy out that part of the business. Armed with a powerful incentive and an extremely hard work ethic, Victor managed to gain control of this end of the business in a very short time. Sven was relieved. Now he was able to focus on his primary interest—the many acres of undeveloped row crops that needed his attention. Sven and Victor both remained independent in their farming interests but had a close relationship over the years.

Nils and Linnea listened intently to Victor's story but couldn't stifle their yawns and fatigue. It was difficult to catch up on all the lost time in one evening and the children had to be put to bed. Shortly after dark, the adults followed suit. Victor and his wife were enjoying the company of their relatives but knew that they would soon have to get up at the crack of dawn to start their chores.

Both Nils and Linnea were early risers, but the next morning the crow of the rooster came too soon. The long journey from Tampa to Piper City had finally begun to take its toll. They could easily have slept for a few more hours.

But the smell of fresh coffee, sizzling bacon and the aroma of freshly baked bread was incentive enough for Nils and Linnea to overcome their lethargy. They quickly got dressed and when they walked onto the kitchen Emma was in the midst of making Swedish pancakes and tending to a pan of fried eggs and bacon. Linnea peered out the window and to her surprise saw her children following their uncle Victor and his other daughter, Mardel as they did their early morning chores. What Linnea didn't realize was that Asta and Sigrid had already helped feed the chickens, watched as Victor milked the cows and were on their way to help muck out the stables. Billy was tagging along for the ride but seemed to be mostly interested in throwing sticks for the dogs to fetch.

Watching them, Linnea quickly realized that there was little free time for them to spend with Victor and his family. The demands of the farm kept them busy from sun up to sun down and even though they managed to catch up on lost time during meals and an hour or two at night, Nils was anxious to get going and start his new job in Chicago. She also was beginning to feel that a relative's visit was like fish—after three days it begins to stink. It had been great to see them and now, that they would be living only a short train ride away, they could soon visit again.

Early the next morning, the Vensberg family loaded all their belongings onto the wagon for the return trip to the train station in Piper City. It was now time to leave for—what they thought would be their final destination—the Chicago suburbs.

SIXTEEN

A New Neighborhood

After the great Chicago fire in 1871, many families began to relocate to the suburbs. Oak Park, Illinois, one of the suburbs that had grown steadily to a population of 40,000 over a period of fifty years, was where Nils and Linnea rented their first apartment. The now famous elevated "L" train in Chicago had expanded to a stop at Harlem Avenue in Oak Park, which allowed easy access between the two cities. Lake Street, one of the first paved venues, was the center of downtown Oak Park and had attracted the establishment of well-known department stores such as Marshall Fields, The Fair and Weiboldts. As the traffic increased, many of the surrounding large older homes were slowly being replaced with apartments. These developments had been an important opportunity for Otto as his business focused on road construction and apartment buildings. It was in one of these apartment buildings that Otto had managed to find a small two-bedroom place for Nils and his family. The location was convenient and gave Nils an easy ride to work on the train.

At home with the children, Linnea was left with the task of finding the nearest grocery store, drug store, church and what was most important—an elementary school for the girls. Linnea's new neighbor, Greta Walzinski, was a big help in getting her acquainted with the neighborhood. Greta had lived in or around Chicago her entire life and had spent the last five years in the Oak Park apartment complex. Daughter of Polish immigrants, her grandfather had moved the family from Chicago's inner city to the suburbs following the great Chicago fire.

Greta soon realized that Linnea's biggest concern was finding a proper school for the girls plus a church for the family and, while taking Linnea around to see the local grocer, butcher and baker, she came up with a terrific suggestion for the girls. "Please forgive me, and I don't mean to pry", Greta inquired, "but since you are from Sweden I assume that you are protestant?"

"I don't mind at all Greta", Linnea answered with a smile. "We are…and I would really like to find a church again. We missed going as a family while we lived in Florida

…we were just too far away to go on a regular basis.

"But why do you ask?"

"Well, there is a Lutheran church not too far from us in Forest Park on the corner of Augusta and Belleforte that also sponsors a school house next door," Greta explained. "I think it would be perfect for your two girls and, if you like, I could take you there tomorrow afternoon!"

"Oh that would be wonderful", Linnea said. "Thanks so much, you have been so kind and helpful."

Linnea was encouraged by the information that Greta had given her, and was anxious to discuss the day's events with Nils when he returned from work that evening. Nils, who was an avid reader, was well aware of the new direction the educational system was taking in Illinois under the influence of Chicago's educational leaders—Francis Parker and John Dewey. They were promoters of a new "progressive" educational system, which proposed a more informal and liberal approach to the classroom. It was in sharp contrast to the more traditional authoritarian methods of the day and instead proposed a curriculum more suited to the individual needs of each student. This new approach was slowly being instituted and widely accepted across much of the country. Nils, on the other hand, was a very strict old-school traditionalist and did not approve in any shape or form of the proposed new methods. For him, the straightforward and simple reading, writing and arithmetic curriculum coupled with a healthy dose of discipline was the only one that worked. Nils was adamant that his children be educated in this manner and not subjected to some new unproven theoretical system.

When Linnea told him that evening of the small Lutheran school that Greta mentioned, he was elated with the idea. "Linnea, that sounds wonderful" Nils replied. "This could be a perfect fit. It'd also be nice to get the family back into the routine of Sunday morning church…I'll be anxious to hear the details after your visit with the Pastor and the schoolteacher. But for now, let's eat and talk with the girls at the dinner table."

Early the next morning, Linnea got the girls and little Billy ready for a walk with Greta to the Grace Evangelical Lutheran Church in Forest Park. The one room Lutheran schoolhouse was next door so it would be easy to meet with both the pastor and the schoolteacher the same day. Although it was early morning, the summer day was already beginning to prove hot and muggy and the elm trees that lined the streets were alive with the loud, steady chorus of the seventeen-year locusts that covered them this year.

It was a pleasant walk with purple lilacs and tulips of

every color in full bloom along the streets, but it was slow going. Little Billy constantly wandered away to chase squirrels or explore someone's backyard. They wound up half-carrying and half-dragging him for most of the last few blocks.

The church was a sparsely landscaped small red brick building with an unusually tall steeple. Typical of the day, it had elongated windows that could be opened from both top and bottom on two exterior walls. This was the most efficient way to cool the building during the hot summer. Greta confidently led them up the front steps and opened the heavy wooden double doors. Inside was a simply adorned main room with straight-backed wooden pews that would accommodate about seventy-five worshipers.

As soon as the front doors opened, Pastor Otto Geisman emerged from his office and hurried towards Greta, Linnea and the family. He was a man on a mission. It was clear that this stout young man with short brown hair and a moustache to match was eager to greet them. A wide smile spread across his pock marked face as he gave an authoritative, "Welcome everyone, it's so very nice to meet you. I am Pastor Geisman."

Offering his hand, he went on to tell them that he had heard of Linnea, Nils and the children through his con-versations with Greta and hoped that they would get to know each other better that day.

Otto Geisman was the fourth Pastor of the Church since its inception in 1904. Born in Sioux City, Iowa he had graduated from Concordia Seminary in St. Louis, Missouri in 1915. After a two-year stay as assistant pastor in Wenona, Illinois and another two years in Pekin, Illinois, he was abruptly summoned to lead the Grace Luteran Church in River Forest to replace Pastor H.C. Englebrecht, who had resigned. Pastor Englebrecht was a German immigrant who, under pressure from the local community, resigned because of heavy anti-German sentiment following World Ward 1. Otto Geisman was also of German descent, but was born in the United States and thought to be less of a target.

He spent the better part of an hour with Linnea and the children, asking them about their previous church experience, schooling, and where they had lived prior to arriving in Oak Park. Linnea quickly became comfortable with his easy-going personality and admired how well he held the attention of the girls.

Sensing that they'd heard enough, Pastor Geisman said, "I don't want to take up too much of your time. If you have any questions please feel free to visit with me at any time and I hope that I will be able to meet with Nils after this Sunday's service. Miss Margaret Heidelberg, our school's teacher, is waiting for us next door, so let's take a walk and I will make the introductions."

The local community of Lutheran families, in order to provide their children with an education more attuned to their heritage, had erected the one room schoolhouse in 1895. At the time it was built, the main road was Harlem Avenue, which was not yet paved. The location of the schoolhouse next to the church made it possible for the children to avoid slogging through the often-muddy condition of Harlem Avenue.

When they entered the schoolhouse, Miss Heidelberg was waiting to greet them. She was in her early thirties, stood about five two and looked to weigh something south of a hundred pounds. Despite the warm summer weather, she wore a long sleeved black dress buttoned snugly up to her neck with thick black shoes to match. Dark brown stockings covered her ankles and feet—the only skin exposed was her hands and face. Her mousy brown hair was pulled so tightly in a bun that, at times, she appeared to have a constant squint. She wore silver horn-rimmed glasses and there was not a hint of makeup to be found—her face a pasty white. She tried her best to smile, as the group and the Pastor entered the room, but you could tell that it didn't come easy to her. Linnea took one look at Miss Heidelberg and thought *this is a woman who means business!* The girls, however, had their stomachs churning with fear as they knew, right away, that school was not going to be much fun.

"Everyone, may I introduce our school's teacher Miss Margaret Heidelberg," the Pastor began. "Miss Heidelberg you, of course, know Greta, and this is a family new to our community—Linnea Vensberg, her daughters Sigrid and Asta and their little brother Billy. I'll leave Miss Heidelberg to explain about the school's hours, curriculum, books, etc., as I need to return to my office and finish writing my sermon for Sunday. Again, it was a pleasure to meet all of you and I look forward to seeing the family in church this Sunday."

Greta took Billy by the hand and volunteered," I'll just take him outside for a while and give you a chance to talk." Margaret gave a sigh of relief as Billy had already broken away running between the wooden desks and was caught, as he was about to scribble on the blackboard with a piece of chalk he had found on the floor.

Miss Heidelberg explained that the school year would begin the day after Labor Day and end the first week in June. Eighteen students were expected to return this year, and now it would be twenty with the addition of Asta and Sigrid. The students ranged in age from seven to fourteen years old. Miss Heidelberg stood in front of her desk. Against the wall to her right, was a long wooden recital bench and on her left was the door to the cloakroom. Behind her was a large blackboard with an American flag on one side of it and a picture of George Washington on the other. The four rows of desks were all firmly bolted to the floor so the students could not move them. A pot-bellied stove at the back of the room heated the schoolhouse and warmed the students' lunches. Alongside the stove was a small square wooden table on top of which sat a large porcelain bowl with a tin cup that served as drinking water during breaks in the day.

She then went on to meticulously describe the daily routine. School was to begin promptly at 9:00 A.M. with the students standing beside their desks. Tardiness would not be tolerated and those who were late would have to stay after class and wash the blackboard, clean out the stove and do whatever chores deemed necessary by the teacher. While still standing they would recite the pledge of allegiance and then sing a hymn (usually "Onward Christian Soldiers"). They would then sit and listen to the teacher read a passage from the bible. Following that, reading lessons would begin with each grade required to sit at the recitation bench and recite to the teacher while the others continued studying their McGuffy readers. This was the only book required and could be purchased at almost any drugstore. All other work would be done on slates. Next followed writing, spelling and penmanship. The later was of particular importance to Miss Heidelberg, as she taught the Palmer method of cursive. Linnea was listening intently to every word and very pleased with what Miss Heidelberg was saying. The girls, on the other hand…not so much. Margaret continued to explain the schedule—short bathroom break (outhouse) and a drink of water, and then arithmetic. Lunch from 11:30 to 12:00 followed by half an hour of some organized games, Pom Pom Pull Away or Tag. In the afternoon it was history, geography and individual help until 4:00 P.M. when class was dismissed.

Miss Heidelberg asked if there were any questions after her talk but as she had been so thorough and detailed, there was very little room for questions. Sensing that she had to say something, Linnea offered, "Thanks so much for your time, we understand everything and I'm sure the girls will look forward to starting school right after Labor Day." Giving the girls a look, they took her cue and said, "Yes Mam! Thank you very much Miss Heidelberg." They tried not to show what they were really thinking, which was, *This woman is scary, and we are really going to have to toe the line!*

On the walk back home Linnea thought to herself, *I am pleased with both the Pastor and Miss Heidelberg, but I hope they won't be too hard on the girls.* Momentarily, she was thrown back in time to the feelings she had about the church back in Sweden, *I hated the strict moralizing of the Lutheran Church…it was one of the reasons I sailed to America!*

Coming back to the present, she realized that, in spite of her misgivings, she was relieved that she could tell Nils that the school would be one more piece of the puzzle that would help give the family a sense of belonging to a community once again.

SEVENTEEN

A Place of Their Own

The summer soon passed with the Vensberg family settling in and growing more accustomed to the lifestyle and weather patterns of the Chicago area. Nils continued to do well at work and developed a strong relationship with Otto and his fellow workers. Otto seemed to line up a never-ending number of construction projects as the U.S. economy began to strengthen following the end of World War I. The Roaring 20's were just beginning to unfold. The girls began school right after Labor Day and discovered that, although Miss Heidelberg was strict in her ways, she was very generous in giving extra time and individual help to the girls with their work. As long as a student was willing to show some interest in their studies, Ms. Heidelberg was more than prepared to give something extra in return. She was especially fond of Siri since she was a quick learner and seemed to be performing above her grade level. It was only a few months into the new school year that Siri managed to skip fourth grade and move into fifth grade level of work.

Nils and Linnea had missed the change of seasons while in Florida, so when the autumn weather came with the leaves changing color and cooler temperatures, they welcomed it. The summer months had been hot and oppressive. They had been accustomed to the winters in Boston but somehow the Chicago winters seemed to be a completely different animal. Beginning in December the strong winds, fueled by Lake Michigan, caused the temperature to drop dramatically and it continued to plummet into late February. The girls had to trudge through the snow each day on their way to school and were grateful that their desks were close to the back of the school room, near the pot-bellied stove. Linnea and Nils were thankful that both girls and Billy had acquired many new friends and were falling into a routine of school, church and play. It gave them all a comfortable sense of kinship.

Meanwhile, Nils began on two new housing projects in River Grove and Elmwood Park. Otto had won a contract with the Polk Brothers realty group to build small one-bedroom houses on several lots that they had developed in that area. Now that the "L" train had a stop in Oak Park and more people were able to afford cars, the suburbs of Chicago were becoming more attractive. The Polk brothers reasoned that by placing a small one-bedroom home in the far back corner of the lot it would make the property appear larger than what it really was. The placement of the house would give many a potential buyer a starter home with plenty of room to expand or rebuild later on.

Nils was attracted to the concept and, with help and encouragement from Otto, he began to think seriously of buying one of the lots in River Grove. He still had some of the money that Otto paid him for the Florida cabin plus a bit more that he had saved since they had arrived in Chicago. He and Linnea both hoped this would be enough for the down payment. The relationship that Otto had with the realtors, and the realtors in turn with the banks, would make the purchase and finance process much easier. What pushed Nils even more rapidly in this direction was the surprise that Linnea was pregnant. The baby was due in December and Nils really wanted to have the family in a home of their own by then. Their current apartment, although comfortable, was on the second floor and Nils did not want Linnea climbing steps during her pregnancy if it could be avoided.

In the spring of 1922, Nils had picked out a property that he liked on Hessing Street in River Grove. It was adjacent to the tracks of The Chicago, Milwaukee and St. Paul Railroad and was priced a bit lower than the other lots on the street because of the noise of passing freight trains. He began negotiations with the Polk Brothers Realty and the local bank with the help of Otto. It all tied neatly together fairly quickly, especially since Otto was able to convince the bank that Nils was a highly skilled and trusted worker who had a long-term future with his company. It took all of Nils's savings but, after agreeing on a final price with the Polk Brothers Realty and another sixty days of paperwork with the bank, the loan was approved and the Vensbergs would finally have a home of their own.

There was no indoor plumbing in the small house so an outhouse was provided about ten yards from the back door. Nils did not want the neighbors to see the family members walking out in the open to the outhouse and he was especially concerned about the cold during the winter months. Consequently, he was not going to move into the new house until he had built a covered walkway connecting the house to the outhouse. It was to be built in such a way that it appeared to be one unified structure. He purchased the wood and other materials to make the roof from Otto, who would leave them at the site for Nils to use on the weekends. Every Saturday and Sunday Nils would walk the eight miles round trip from Oak

Park to Hessing Street in River Grove, to work on his project. It was slow going, working by himself, but he managed to finish over several weekends and the family was finally ready to move on June 15th, 1922. Given the size of the lot and the location of the small house in the far corner, Nils was already envisioning plans for a larger home, positioned in the middle of the property closer to the front street—with indoor plumbing, a basement, and enough bedrooms for everyone.

The children were excited to hear the news that they would be moving into a home they could call their own. School was out for the summer and they looked forward to helping with the move. Even Billy was now old enough to understand that something very special was about to happen. Unfortunately, the move meant the school in Forest Park would be too far away for the girls to continue there. They would have to look for something closer to home in River Grove. Now that Linnea was pregnant, Nils did not want her to have the additional worry of the girls trying to walk the four miles to school. It would be equally as difficult for Linnea to walk the same distance with the family to attend church. It was too much of an imposition on Otto Bendler to take them back and forth in his car, especially on Sunday, which was his only day off. As much as they liked Pastor Geisman, they would have to find a church closer to their new home.

The new home was extremely modest, consisting of one bedroom that would be taken by Linnea and Nils, and a combination living room and kitchen. The kitchen had a water basin that really was nothing more than a cast-iron deep sink. It would serve as a place to alternately wash dishes, clothes, and provide water to bathe. A small wood-burning stove helped to heat the house and was used to cook the daily meals. It would be tight quarters for a while until Nils could manage to build a larger home on the property. For now, that meant that Siri, Asta, and Billy would all have to sleep on the pullout sofa together in the living room—an arrangement that did not sit very well with the girls. Billy was a fitful sleeper, constantly tossing and turning and pulling the covers from the girls. Fights would invariably break out. In her defense, Asta relied on making up stories when they first went to bed. They seemed to hold Billy's attention and keep him from fidgeting. Asta became very creative in her story telling and went on and on until Nils would finally stick open the door to his room and tell Asta to stop and go to sleep.

Each morning the girls had to fold the blankets, put away the sofa bed and in general return the living room to its original state. More often than not, they were also responsible for scrubbing the linoleum-covered floor with a stiff brush while down on their hands and knees. There was no running water in the house so Siri and Asta had to go down to the Ellerson house one block away where there was a well. Several trips with metal buckets provided the family with enough water to scrub the floors and fill up the basin for cooking and washing. It was a routine that had to be done every single day.

During the remainder of the summer months, the children found time after their chores to make friends with the rest of the kids on the block. It seemed that everyone they met had a similar background—parents who had emigrated at different times from Europe and finally settled in River Grove. This wasn't unusual, as more than fifty percent of the River Grove population at the time was either foreign born or of foreign parentage. Perhaps the most interesting, however, was their immediate neighbor Mrs. P. who was one of the first to buy a home on Hessing Street. She was a fifty-three year-old widow with no children and rumored to be related to the Guggenheim family by those that had lived on the street for some time. She was somewhat of an eccentric, who usually kept to herself, but almost inexplicably, took an immediate liking to the Vensberg family. She quickly determined that Linnea had no interest in prying into her personal life or affairs and just wanted to be a friendly neighbor. Unlike the rest of the ruffians on the block, as she called them, Mrs. P.

also found Siri and Asta to be very polite and well behaved. For that reason, she quickly developed a close relationship with Linnea that allowed her, at times, to share some of her personal past.

Day by day and week-by-week Nils and Linnea began to acquaint themselves with everyone that lived on Hessing Street. Their other immediate neighbor was the Barto family. Mr. and Mrs. Barto were from Sicily and spoke with a thick Italian accent. They had three children—Alfred, Emil, and Sarah—all of whom matched up close enough in age to the Vensberg kids. They quickly became good friends. They would help each other carry water from the Ellerson's well each day and after their chores were done play Pom Pom Pull Away, Kick the Can or ice skate on the river during the winter. Mr. Barto was a tough disciplinarian from the old country and had a strict code of morality. Unfortunately, none of it seemed to rub off on his son. Alfred was as mischievous as they come, a trait that constantly amused both Asta and Siri. If Billy had been the same age he probably would have been the perfect accomplice to Alfred.

Once a month the "rag man" man would come to the neighborhood in his truck to buy old rags, bottles and in general anything unwanted lying around the house. He would stand in front of his truck and negotiate a price for rags and bottles after which he would toss them into the back of the truck. Alfred just simply could not help himself. While the ragman was in the front of his truck haggling over price, Alfred was in the back of the truck helping himself to the already purchased merchandise. He would then get back in line and sell the stolen rags to the man for the second time. The girls could only shake their heads in amazement at Alfred's brazen antics.

The remainder of the neighborhood, as one went down the street towards Grand Avenue, included the Ellersons (German), the Lorentsons (Swedish), Petersens (Norwegian), Stephans (Polish) and the Lendalls (English). There were actually two families of Ellersons on the block, both of whom encouraged Nils and Linnea to attend their church-—the Bethlehem Lutheran Church on Oak Street. It was much the same as the church they attended in River Forest and it also had a one-room schoolhouse located on the same property. The girls would need to start school again in a couple of months so this seemed to be a perfect fit.

On a warm Sunday morning in July, the entire Vensberg family, accompanied by the Ellersons, walked the half-mile to the Church on Oak Street to attend the service and later meet with the Pastor to learn more of the school for Siri and Asta.

Asta and Siri went with the Ellerson girls to Sunday

school, which was taught by the older high school girls in the one-room school house at the back of the church, while Nils and Linnea attended the service. Billy miraculously sat quietly on Linnea's lap during most of the service. He seemed to be fascinated with the music and the colors of the stained glass windows. However, Linnea sat strategically at the end of the pew so she could remove Billy if he acted up. Fortunately she only had to take him outside once for a short break, which was quite remarkable, considering the length of the service.

After the service, the Vensbergs were to meet with the head of the church in the schoolhouse. The Ellersons began to walk home, as they wanted to make sure that Nils, Linnea and the girls had some time alone with the Pastor. They offered to take Billy with them, which turned out to be a good idea as he was hot and tired from sitting so long. The girls found the schoolhouse very similar to their school in River Forest, although a bit larger. The teacher's desk in front, recitation bench, cloakroom, pot-bellied stove, etc. were all pretty much the same.

The Pastor walked into the room still dressed in his black robe with his clergyman's collar tightly wrapped around his thin neck. He was a slight man of average height, short black hair and large round green eyes. He had come to the church in 1919, with all the very old-school German Lutheran traditions.

Up until the beginning of World War I, all of the services and meetings were held only in German. This was typical of most German Lutheran Churches. It was a consensus among the German settlers that English was a crude language that would not allow for a proper understanding of theology. He was a firm believer of this theory and clung to the old ways of the church. He was extremely disappointed when German began to slowly disappear from the Lutheran Church as a result of the anti-German sentiment as the US entered the war against Kaiser Wilhelm's regime.

Standing erect with his hands behind his back, he began to address them in his slight German accent, "As you already know from the service today I am the Reverend of this church, but what you probably don't know is that I also serve as the school's teacher."

The announcement came as a surprise to both Nils and Linnea. The girls were visibly taken aback, although they tried not to show it. What they sensed was…this was not good.

"I know from the Ellersons that you attended the River Forest School this past year with Miss Heidelberg", he began. "Our curricula are very much the same, with the exception of some time set aside to teach German. I think you will find the routine very similar to Miss Heidelberg's. As usual, we will begin classes the day after Labor Day. I look forward to seeing you then. Class will start promptly each day at 9:00 A.M. and end at 4:00 P.M. If you don't have any questions, it was very nice to have met you and good afternoon," he said with a slight bow, never offering his hand. Even if they had a question or two, it would have been too uncomfortable to ask. Both parties could not wait to leave.

During the walk home Linnea asked Nils, "So what did you think?"

His immediate response was, "If you're asking me about the Reverend's personality then that's difficult to say…I didn't notice it. That is…if he has one! I felt a little like we were back in Sweden! The sermon was all right and I am sure the school will be good for the girls, but he's not the type I'd care to get very close to. He seemed very unfriendly…did you notice that he didn't even offer to shake my hand?"

Linnea had to admit that the Pastor did not exactly exude the usual warm and comfortable feeling normally associated with a clergyman. Not wanting to continue on with the subject she said, "Well we will just have to make the best of it for now and hope the girls will make some new friends." That seemed to end the conversation and they all walked home.

EIGHTEEN

A New Arrival

Linnea's pregnancy had gone without any problems for eight months. Outside of a few bouts of morning sickness during the first few weeks, she had not experienced any complications. It was November and the temperature was dropping steadily with each passing day. Their wood-burning stove, however, managed to keep their small home nice and toasty. The girls had become accustomed to their new school and slowly began to make new friends. As expected, the Reverend was a strict disciplinarian but both Siri and Asta managed to keep their heads down, obey the rules and carry out their lessons. Nils was constantly asking them about school to see if he could detect any mistreatment. Ever since his first encounter with the Reverend, he worried that he was too strict, but they continued to go to church every Sunday. It was a conveniently short walk from their house, and Nils felt compelled to keep his family close to their faith.

As the Chicago suburbs continued to expand, so did Otto Bender's business. Nils had plenty of work and was quickly becoming comfortable with the process of building houses and apartments. He was an accomplished cabinet-maker and carpenter by trade, but now he had to learn the practice of framing walls, foundation construction, plumbing and masonry. He was eager to learn these skills as the intent to build a larger house on his property was becoming more urgent. Linnea was soon to give birth which would now mean a family of six crowded into their small home. He would not be able to start construction until spring when the snow had cleared but it did not prevent him from putting his ideas for the new house on paper. Each night Nils would continue to sketch out the plans for the house. There would be many revisions before the actual construction would begin in the spring of 1923, but in the meantime it was a project that kept them both happily occupied during the winter. Linnea loved participating in the planning and often had ideas that hadn't occurred to Nils.

It was on one of those nights, with the snow falling heavily outside, while they were discussing the location of the bathroom for the new house, that Linnea felt the contractions coming on. As she moved to lie down on their bed, she anxiously looked at Nils and announced, "This baby is coming soon and I don't think we will have time to make it to a hospital."

Nils immediately sprang into action and comforted Linnea by saying, "Now, not to worry. You just try to relax, breathe deeply and leave everything to me." He opened the door to the small living room where the children were sleeping and gently woke them up.

Quickly he announced, "Your mother is about to have the baby. Siri you need to warm up some water on the stove. Asta please gather some clean bed sheets and rags. Afterward you need to go next door and tell Mrs. P. what is happening and ask her if she wouldn't mind coming over to help. Siri, you keep an eye on Billy while Asta fetches Mrs. P." Excitedly the girls began to do as they were told. Meanwhile Nils returned to their bed where he held Linnea's hand. He tried his best to comfort her with a damp cloth that he had dipped into the water basin and continued to give instructions to the children.

"How's the pain? I have sent Asta next door to get Mrs. P. just in case we need some help" Nils said, trying to reassure her. Linnea could only give a brief nod of approval before she winced at yet another oncoming contraction. As the pain slowly began to subside, there was a slight knock on door of the bedroom. Nils opened the door just enough to see Mrs. P. on the other side.

"I came as quickly as I could. Is there anything I can do?"

"Thanks so much for coming Mrs. P. I think it would be a big help to me if you could just watch over the children for now. I'll let you know if I need some help", Nils explained.

Less than twenty minutes later Mrs. P. and the children heard the loud cry of a baby from the bedroom. Nils was all smiles as he opened the door and poked his head out to proudly announce, "Siri, Asta, Billy…you have a new baby sister!! Fat and sassy!! Mrs. P. I think you can come in now and maybe help me clean up a bit." Meanwhile, the children were all jumping up and down with excitement celebrating the birth of their new baby sister who was to be named Ida Margaret Vensberg, born on December 5th 1922.

Everything had happened so rapidly that they had not given much thought as to where the baby would sleep. Linnea, the master of improvisation, quickly remedied the situation with a trunk at the foot of their bed that had traveled with her from Sweden. Opening the lid, she arranged a soft blanket in its now concave shape. This would be baby Ida's bed until they could make more permanent arrangements.

NINETEEN

Let the Building Begin!

In early March of 1923 Nils began to stockpile materials that he would need to begin construction of his main house. He wanted to be ready for the first sign of spring when the snow had melted and the ground would be soft enough to dig out the basement and foundation. Otto was more than generous in providing some extra materials such as cinder blocks and cement left over from his housing projects. By mid-April the temperatures began to rise. The end of the winter was near and Nils looked forward to digging the foundation of his new house. He would need the help of some machinery and Otto was happy to provide it—especially since he was currently working on an apartment complex not too far away from Nils's home. It took several weeks for them to excavate the basement area but, once it was done, Nils was determined to finish the rest of the house on his own.

Providing it did not rain, Nils spent every free moment working on the house. He set up wide wooden planks that reached from the ground level down into the dugout basement bottom. Siri and Asta would slide cinder blocks down the wooden planks to Nils who was waiting to retrieve them at what would soon be the basement floor. With cement, sand and water, handed down to him in pails on a rope by Siri and Asta, Nils would mix these elements in his wheelbarrow and, one by one, cement the cinder blocks in place to form the walls of the basement. It was slow and tedious work for both Nils and the girls but they all had the motivation to keep on. Nils was driven to finish so that his growing family could be more comfortable and the girls were looking forward to having a room and bed of their own. For them, it was getting more and more difficult to get a good night sleep with Billy in the same bed. Asta was also running out of stories to tell at night.

This routine went on month after month until November when winter set in again. It was impossible to work outside anymore. But by November, Nils had managed to complete all four walls of the basement and tie them together by pouring the cement floor. It was much less than he had expected to get done, given the amount of time he spent on the foundation, but it was a good start and hopefully he could begin on the main floor next spring. He figured that once he had the main floor down, he could start to frame up the outside walls and continue to work, at least sporadically, during the next winter.

The Vensberg family in front of the smaller home.
L to R: Siri, Asta, Linnea, "Mickey", Billy, and Nils

The girls had been a huge help, although Nils tried to give them some free time to enjoy the summer. It was back breaking work for Nils considering his regular construction job with Otto which was just as demanding. In effect he was working seven days a week.

The baby, now affectionately called Mickey, was almost

a year old and thriving on the attention she got from the whole family. The age difference was such that the girls could play "Mother" as they took care of little Mickey. This gave Linnea more time for cooking, washing clothes, sewing and making sure Nils had a decent lunch pail of food to take to work each day. The only one a bit resentful was Billy, as he was no longer the center of attention as the youngest in the family. He was always somewhat rebellious and single-minded so it probably only strengthened his resolve to be independent.

Meanwhile, the U.S. economy was growing strong and that helped Otto's business, which in turn kept Nils employed, and his family comfortable. The "Roaring Twenties" were in full swing. The auto industry continued to grow, and electrical and telephone services were reaching many more homes. There was an upsurge in construction of palatial movie theaters, nightclubs and large sports stadiums. It seemed to many that the economy was on an upward trend, one that would continue indefinitely. It was a belief that would soon prove to be false.

TWENTY

The Big Move

The first indication of trouble on the horizon for the U.S. was a Florida hurricane. On September 18, 1926, one of the most destructive hurricanes to hit the U.S. blew through the Fort Lauderdale-Miami area with winds of more than 150 mph. At the time there was a very primitive advanced warning system, and few people had radios to hear the broadcast warnings. In addition, most of the population at the time was made up of new landowners from the northern states. They were totally unfamiliar with, and unprepared for, the power of a hurricane. An estimated eight hundred people died and every building in Miami was either damaged or completely destroyed.

This event put an abrupt halt to the land boom in Florida. Most of those who had invested in property there were from the northern states and, after witnessing the destruction of the storm, walked away from their heavily leveraged loans. The banks were left holding the bag. Many others, who were potential investors, began to look elsewhere to put their money. Property values in Florida plummeted and the banks were no longer interested in lending against the declining property values. Unfortunately, even though Tampa suffered only minor damage, Otto was also a financial victim. The value of his property dropped severely and any hope he had of selling at a profit in the near future was gone.

Nils was sorry to hear of Otto's troubles in Florida, but was also intent on finishing their new home. Finally, in October of 1926, after nearly three and a half years of construction, they moved into the house. Although the roof was finished, the rafters were still exposed and some rooms in the house remained without a ceiling. Linnea was not entirely in agreement with the move as winter was fast approaching and she did not think Nils would have time to put up the remaining ceiling and insulate them from the oncoming cold. But Nils was not to be stopped by the weather…he was anxious to move into this house that had taken so much time and effort to build. Chicago temperatures were still mild, and he figured that he had plenty of time to finish the rest of the ceiling and insulation before the cold weather arrived.

On a balmy October day, with the help of the neighbors, Nils and his family moved their meager possessions into the new house. It was against Linnea's better judgment and she kept reminding Nils, "I don't think this is such a good idea. What's the rush? The house is not finished yet and what if the cold weather comes sooner this year?"

The Vensberg Home built by Nils circa 1928

Nils would counter with, "Linnea, you worry too much. Everything will be just fine. I don't want to wait until the spring to move in. It will only take me a few weeks before I finish up the ceiling and insulation. Besides look at the beautiful weather we are having." The children, however, were oblivious to their parents' concerns and were eager and excited to claim territory in their new bedrooms. Siri and Asta had been waiting for a long time to have a bedroom of their own without the nuisance of little Billy. Siri had just turned fourteen and Asta twelve, and they were looking forward to being separated from their brother. They would sleep, for the time being, in the same bed since Nils did not have enough money to buy more furniture. He had sunk every last penny into the new house. But it was such an improvement for the girls to have their own room, however, they did not mind sharing a bed. Mickey would be four years old in December and was now too big to be sleeping in the same room as Linnea and Nils. Much to the disappointment of Billy, he would have to share the third bedroom with his little sister.

The move did not take long, which left most of the afternoon to celebrate with the neighbors. Linnea did not have time to cook on moving day so everyone on the street brought over food and drink. Mrs. Barto made a mountain of ravioli, the Ellerson's brought German potato salad, the Stephans, polish sausage and the Lorentsons provided some fig wine. Mr. Ellerson brought over his concertina to provide some music as they all joined in singing songs of their home countries.

By mid-afternoon all the neighbors began to head home.

The last to leave was the Barto family who were in the process of collecting their now empty large bowl that only hours ago held an enormous amount of ravioli. Nils and Linnea decided to walk outside with them to say good-bye. As they opened the door the cold air rushed in. The sky was turning grey and the wind was beginning to pick up. There was no reason to speak as the chilly look that Linnea gave Nils said more than enough. Celia Barto confirmed the worst as she announced, "Oh my, but the weather has turned in a hurry. The temperature must have dropped twenty degrees in the past couple of hours. Come on now Harold, let's be on our way and let the Vensbergs get back inside."

Once back inside, Linnea gave a look toward Nils with which he was all too familiar. It was her unmistakable "I told you so!" look. Nils could only try and preempt what was surely coming. "I know what you're thinking, but trust me, we will all be just fine. I will crank up the furnace and cover the children with extra blankets. We will all be warm as toast," he tried to say with some conviction.

The only truth in his statement was that there was indeed enough coal to stoke the furnace. Siri and Asta were used to pulling their wagon down to the train tracks almost every day to collect coal that would fall from the coal train on its way into Chicago. The cars of the train numbered well over a hundred and were filled to the brim. Some of the coal would invariably fall alongside the tracks. Many times the train would stop at the station at the end of their street and wait to switch to another track. The conductor, when he noticed the girls were there alongside the tracks, would order the coal tender to shovel some coal down to the girls. All was done with a wave and a smile from the conductor who couldn't talk over the noise of the steam engine. Over the past several months, the girls had managed to stockpile an impressive amount of coal in the backyard that would last through most of the winter.

It was now dark outside and the temperature began to drop even more rapidly. Nils went down to the basement and feverishly stoked the furnace; he also checked on the valves leading to the radiators that were placed throughout the house. Linnea began to put the children to bed, distributing as many extra blankets as she could find. The wind now began to howl through the open rafters and all of the radiators began to clang and bang as they struggled to provide heat to the house. Nils had never tested the heating system and struggled to balance the radiators as some of the valves seemed to be stuck half open. By now, the combination of cold, wind, and clanging of the radiators had Asta almost in tears. Siri tried her best to comfort her. It was more of the same with Billy and little

Mickey as Nils seemed to be running out of ideas to manufacture more heat. This was not how he had envisioned his first night in the new house.

Throughout the ordeal and mayhem, Linnea's silence spoke louder than words to poor Nils who had now given up for the night on fixing the heating system. Ironically, the bigger house with all of its extra bedrooms was reduced to the same size as their small house because everyone had to move into the bedroom of Nils and Linnea to stay warm.

TWENTY-ONE

Summer Break

Under the threat from Linnea to move back into the small house, Nils woke up the next morning earlier than usual. He knew only too well that Linnea would not give him much time to fix the heating problem and there would not be peace until then. At work on the job site, Nils was able to commandeer the help of a plumber who agreed to come take a look at the heating system after work. Fortunately, the problem seemed to be limited to replacing a few valves and balancing off the radiators.

With the heating problem solved, the family was finally able to enjoy their new living quarters and peace reigned over the household once again. Over the next several weeks, Nils was able to enclose the open rafters. He could now concentrate on some of the detail work at his own pace.

Always thinking ahead, and never able to rest, Nils was already on to his next project—building a garage. Although the family still did not have a car, Nils could not keep still and was determined to put up a garage with enough space to set up a small workshop and room to store his tools. Now that Linnea was convinced that the big house was going to be permanent, Nils planned to tear down the little house in the back of the lot and in its place construct the garage or "garage and a half" as he liked to call it. But with winter coming soon he would have to put off his project again until the spring.

Siri was now in her first year at Leyden High School in River Grove. Asta was in seventh grade and little Billy in third, both of them still in the one room schoolhouse at the Grace Evangelical Lutheran. The Reverend had resigned as schoolmaster due to ill health, but remained as church pastor. Asta was relieved, and both children were happy with his replacement.

As the summer of 1927 approached, the girls were eagerly anticipating the end of the school year and summer vacation. They had been such a big help with the construction of the new house and taking care of little Mickey during the past year that Nils and Linnea decided to reward them with a trip to Uncle Victor's farm in Piper City. Taking the train all by themselves to Piper city was about as good as it gets for

Siri and Asta. They could not wait for their two-week adventure on the farm. They fondly remembered their brief visit on their way to Chicago. The wide open country surroundings, the farm animals, fresh eggs, milk, and the aroma of hot biscuits were all still very fresh in their memories.

Unfortunately, the train ride was the only memorable event of their summer vacation that year. Uncle Victor had no time for leisurely visits and immediately put the girls to work. They started the day at the break of dawn. They were not served breakfast, as they had anticipated, but rather were expected to make it not only for themselves but for the farm hands as well. After breakfast, they had to feed the chickens, then the hogs, and help milk the cows. When noon approached, it was back in the kitchen to help Emma prepare lunch for everyone, including the farm hands. In the afternoon, they went directly to the barn where they were to clean the stalls, provide fresh hay for the plow horses and bring water from the well to the feeding trough. By the time the dinner hour arrived, they were pretty much exhausted.

The routine varied little over the next two weeks. The free time they had was limited to the few hours after dinner before going to bed. The only thing they were grateful for was the company of each other and the fact that they could at least commiserate about their "vacation" on the farm. They missed home and their little brother and sister, but most of all the fun times they would have together. It was so different from the life style of Uncle Victor and his family. Both Siri and Asta were used to hard work. At home, they helped around the house scrubbing floors, washing clothes, bringing water from the well, collecting coal around the railroad tracks, taking care of little Mickey on the weekends and doing homework from school. They had become accustomed to that and never complained. But when all was said and done the evenings were always reserved for family time. Nils would play his violin or teach the girls how to play the piano and they would always end up singing songs together. Nils never lost his passion for singing especially from his experience with the Swedish Choral Society while they were in Boston. Little Billy seemed to have inherited his father's ability for singing. He had a good musical ear and loved to sing. His voice was mature beyond his years.

When the girls returned from Uncle Victor's farm they did not want to disappoint their parents who had sacrificed so much to send them away for the two weeks that they told stories of their experience on the farm that were generally cheerful. They were careful not to divulge their true feelings. Nils and Linnea were delighted and responded with promises that, hopefully, they could send them again next summer. Siri and Asta could only try and muster a weak smile in return. They both dreaded the thought of returning to the Piper City farm.

TWENTY-TWO

A Commitment to Stay

Sometime before finishing construction of the house, Nils had made a decision to apply for U.S. citizenship. Since his arrival in Boston, he had married Linnea, made steady economic progress (albeit a bit choppy at times), had four healthy children, a home, some property and a good job. He reasoned, along with Linnea's encouragement, that it was time to make the commitment to his family and the country that had given him so many opportunities. His instinct from the very beginning was that his stay in the U.S. would be permanent with little likelihood of returning to Sweden. The Vensbergs had completely embraced the American way of life and now Nils wanted to make sure that his children were not handicapped in any way by their parents being insensitively labeled as immigrants.

The Immigration and Naturalization Service (INS) facilitated the naturalization process in the 1920's. This bureau was created with the intent to provide some standardization to the naturalization process. The U.S. judicial system or clerk of court accepted all applications for citizenship and ultimately a judge gave the final approval for naturalization. Prior to the creation of the INS, however, there was no real uniformity to the examination process to gain citizenship. For the most part, immigrants would use a wide variety of at-home study guides that were supposed to prepare them for the hearings at the naturalization courts. It was entirely at the discretion of the judge to ask whatever questions he deemed necessary as well as determine their proficiency, or lack thereof, in English.

Nils was the first of his neighborhood to apply for citizenship, and true to his nature, carefully researched the steps necessary to become a naturalized citizen. The first requirement was to file a declaration of intent with the clerk of court located in downtown Chicago. In December of 1925, Nils took the "L" train from the Harlem Avenue station in Oak Park to downtown Chicago. At the court, Nils paid the one-dollar application fee and took an oath of his bona fide intent to become a U.S. citizen, to reside permanently therein, and renounce all allegiances to other nations. It was a huge first step, but one that Nils was firmly committed to taking.

Now that Nils had made the initial application he would have to wait the mandatory two years before he could petition the court for citizenship. Due to the flood of applications, however, there was such a backlog in the court system that it could take anywhere from two to seven years before obtaining citizenship. The INS was created to alleviate such delays but it would take years before they were able to speed up the process. One of the ways the INS was able to accelerate the procedure was the implementation of government supported night schools available to citizenship applicants in their communities. There they could improve their English and study the fundamentals of U.S. Government and its history.

Through the help of Siri, Nils arranged to start a night school course for citizenship given at Leyden High School. He would walk the six miles round trip once a week for two years to attend the night school at Leyden High School. Nils would study…and study…and study some more. The textbook used at the time was called "The Federal Citizens Textbook" which was a hundred and sixty eight pages long divided into a hundred and twenty five chapters.

The first fifty chapters dealt with the English language: vocabulary, pronunciation, writing, spelling and grammar. Nils had a fairly good understanding of the language and could have easily skipped through several of the chapters but, instead, he worked his way through all of them with the rest of the group. The next fifty chapters dealt with a variety of practical subjects such as how to lease an apartment, use the library and post office, how to write a check, first aid, the importance of cooking food properly, etc. The last chapters encompassed American Government and Civics; the Constitution, Bill of Rights, balance of power, elections, voting rights, etc. This was probably the most intense part of the textbook and the one that interested Nils the most.

After more than two years of study, one evening the instructor at school announced that the INS examiner would be coming to interview and question those applicants who felt they were ready to be approved to receive their U.S. citizenship. Nils had studied hard and often, reading at public libraries about the U.S. government on those days when night school was not in session. He could have met with the examiner much earlier but was forced to wait until his particular night school was on the schedule.

Nils passed the examiner's questions and interview, leaving him one step closer to citizenship. That next step was to appear in a Chicago court, with two witnesses that could vouch for the applicant's good moral character and attest that he had lived in the United States for more than five years. Otto and his brother were more than happy to take Nils to the downtown Chicago courthouse to vouch for him. Nils paid four dollars for that application and now had only to wait for a letter asking him to appear before a judge.

It was February 7th, 1928 when Nils appeared at the court for what he hoped would be the final phase of the naturalization process. Judge Robert B. Smith was presiding over the court. Normally, the certificate given by the INS examiner for completion of the night school course was sufficient for the court to approve citizenship. Even though Nils had his certificate, legally, the final approval was still left up to the courts. Judge Smith always used this option to choose one of the candidates at random for a one on one final examination. Nils was the "lucky" one that day—he was selected for the one on one.

Judge Smith came from a lineage that probably could be traced back to the pilgrims that landed on Plymouth Rock. His father was born in America, as was his grandfather, great grandfather, and from there as far back as one could go.

He viewed the dramatic increase of immigrants into the United States over the previous thirty years as uncontrolled. He felt it would eventually lead to an erosion of the American life style. Before the inception of the INS, he and the courts were the sole governing body that would determine whether an immigrant qualified for citizenship. He was extremely disappointed that he had to relinquish some of his control over the process to the INS and did everything in his power to stretch the legal rules in his favor in order to diminish the influence of the INS.

With that in mind, Judge Smith looked at Nils standing before him and asked, "So Mr. Vensberg, why is it that you want to become a citizen of the United States?" Nils paused for the longest time, gathering his thoughts in preparation for how he was going to answer the judge's question. After what seemed to be an awkward amount of time, Judge Smith broke the silence, "Mr. Vensberg, did you understand the question or would you like me to repeat it?"

"Oh no, I understood perfectly your honor," Nils responded, "I was just thinking about how I have studied over the past two years hundreds of chapters about how the U.S. government works, its history, the meaning of the flag, the role of the President, and many other facts and figures, but I never really had to study about the question you just asked me. It is really, however, an easy one for me to answer. You see I came to this country with nothing and it, in turn, has given me everything. During the boat trip over to the US, I met my future wife. Not long after, we landed in Boston where we married. Later my four children were born here and I was fortunate enough to find a job that allowed me to practice my trade as a carpenter. Over time I was able to buy some property and build a house of my own with the skills I learned here. It seems to me that some people take for granted the privileges provided by this country. I don't. I am very grateful for what I have and proud of what I have been able to accomplish with the help of my new American friends. I have unconditionally adopted this country and now hope it will officially adopt me."

Now it was Judge Smith that had to pause for a moment, clear his throat and proceed with, "Very well, let's move on. You mentioned that you have studied the U.S. government, the presidents, American history, etc, etc. Tell me a little bit about what you have learned."

Nils responded by explaining the balance of power between the executive, judicial and legislative branches, the meaning of the stars and stripes on the flag, the Declaration of Independence, and he named all of the presidents (in order), and on and on. The judge finally interrupted his recital and asked, "You listed all of our Presidents. Which one is your favorite?"

Without hesitation Nils responded, "Abraham Lincoln your honor."

To which Judge Smith curtly asked, "Why?"

"He delivered the Gettysburg Address, one of our most famous speeches" Nils replied.

Quickly the judge asked, "And what do you know about the Gettysburg Address Mr. Vensberg?"

"Four score and seven years ago…" Nils began to recite.

"No, no, no, no" said the judge, abruptly cutting him off. "You see that is exactly what I don't like about the INS. They teach you to memorize facts and figures, speeches and songs, but fail to teach the meaning of them. What is the meaning of the Gettysburg Address Mr. Vensberg? It is the meaning that I am after."

"I apologize your honor", Nils responded, "I must have misunderstood your question." He gathered himself and continued, "President Lincoln was in office during one of the most difficult times in U.S. history. The civil war had divided the country with a tremendous loss of life. Mr. Lincoln was asked to speak at a memorial service in Gettysburg for those that had died in a battle there. I believe he saw it as an opportunity to try and reunite the country by reminding everyone of the common principles on which this country was founded. That the men that died in this battle were fighting to preserve equality and freedom for all, just as the Declaration of Independence stated."

There was not much more the judge could say. He would

have to look for another candidate to test. Frustrated, Judge Smith announced almost with a bit of resignation, "That will be all Mr. Vensberg. The swearing in ceremony will be at 2:00 P.M. today."

Relieved, Nils addressed the Judge with, "Thank you very much your honor".

Before Nils could turn around and walk out of the courtroom, Judge Smith could not resist having the last word, "Oh, and one last thing Mr. Vensberg—you need to improve your English."

Nils bristled inside at the comment but was not going to let the judge get the best of him. He said under his breath in Swedish, "Well at least I can speak two languages!" as he left the courtroom without ever acknowledging the judge's final comment.

Judge Smith thought he heard something and said, "Mr. Vensberg, what did you just say?"

Thinking quickly, Nils turned around and said, "So sorry your honor, I was just repeating an old Swedish prayer of thanks."

Nils walked out of the courtroom where his two witnessses, Otto and his brother Henry, were anxiously waiting for him.

"So how did it go Nils?" inquired Otto.

Nils smiled and replied, "Well, he told me at the end of the interview, that the swearing in ceremony was at 2.00 P.M. so I assume that I passed. Now let's all get out of here for a while and find a cup of coffee and maybe something to eat."

At 2.00 P.M. about thirty five applicants were ushered into the courtroom where Judge Smith asked them all to raise their hands and pledge allegiance to the United States Constitution and renounce all foreign allegiances. Once that was done Judge Smith issued an official order of admission to citizenship and granted all of them a certificate of citizenship. Normally, that would have been the end of the ceremony but Judge Smith always ended with a little twist.

Judge Smith declared, "Congratulations everyone and now to end the ceremony, and as a reminder why we are all here, I would ask that you face the flag, put your hand over your heart and recite the pledge of allegiance." His next remark took Nils by complete surprise, "Mr. Vensberg, would you mind coming to the front and lead us in the pledge?" A bit stunned, Nils came to the front of the group, put his hand over his heart, and with a steady baritone voice began,

"I pledge allegiance to the flag of the United States of America and to the Republic for which it stands, one nation under God, with liberty and justice for all." When he had finished, they all walked out of the courtroom officially as American Citizens.

The ride back home to River Grove seemed an eternity to Nils, as he was anxious to tell his family and friends the good news. Once Otto turned off of Grand Avenue and onto Hessing Street, he began honking the horn and did not stop until he pulled into the Vensberg driveway. By now everyone in the neighborhood had made their way down the street to see what all the commotion was about. Linnea knew exactly what had happened and was the first to greet Nils with a big hug and a kiss. The children joined the group hug and the neighbors that had gathered let out a big collective cheer as Nils held up his certificate of citizenship high over his head and said, "I am officially a United States Citizen!"

That weekend a neighborhood tradition began with a celebration at the Vensbergs for the new U.S. citizen. It would be one of many such parties, as one by one, with the help and encouragement of Nils and Linnea, the neighbors went to night school in preparation for their citizenship papers. They would rely heavily on both Nils and Linnea to coach them through the process. The biggest word of advice from Nils was that everyone should speak English at every opportunity. It was the language of their new country and was essential if they were to fully understand the laws of the nation, and successfully integrate into this society.

THE UNITED STATES OF AMERICA

CERTIFICATE OF NATURALIZATION

No. 2722463

TO BE GIVEN TO THE PERSON NATURALIZED.

Petition, Volume 286 Number 46968

Description of holder: Age 42 years; height 5 feet, 8 inches; color White; complexion, Dark; color of eyes, Blue Gray; color of hair, Brown; visible distinguishing marks, None

Name, age and place of residence of wife:

(NOTE.—AFTER SEPTEMBER 22, 1922, HUSBAND'S NATURALIZATION DOES NOT MAKE WIFE A CITIZEN.)

Names, ages and places of residence of minor children: Sigrid age 15 years; Astrid age 13 years; John age 9 years; and Ida age 5 years; River Grove, Illinois

ORIGINAL

UNITED STATES OF AMERICA
NORTHERN DISTRICT OF ILLINOIS } SS:

Be it remembered, that NILS FERDINAND VENSBERG then residing at number 2623 Hessing Street, Town of River Grove, State of Illinois, who previous to his naturalization was a subject of SWEDEN, having applied to be admitted a citizen of the United States of America pursuant to law and at a Regular term of the District Court of the United States held at Chicago, on the 7th day of February, in the year of our Lord nineteen hundred and 28, the court having found that the petitioner intends to reside permanently in the United States, and that he had, in all respects, complied with the Naturalization Laws of the United States, and that he was entitled to be so admitted, it was thereupon ordered by the said court that he be admitted as a citizen of the United States of America.

In testimony whereof the seal of said court is hereunto affixed on the 7th day of February in the year of our Lord nineteen hundred and 28, and of our Independence the one hundred and fifty-second.

[SEAL]

Clerk, District Court of the United States,
Northern District of Illinois.
(Official character of attester)

DEPARTMENT OF LABOR

A party was held in the Vensberg's basement where they had plenty of room to dance to the music played by Mr. Ellerson on his concertina. Everyone brought their favorite dishes spread out all over the kitchen on trays. The Barto's ravioli, the Lendall's Shepard's Pie, the Stephans's Polish sausage and bread, and of course Linnea, who made Swedish meatballs. In a corner of the basement was a vat of fig wine that Nils had made. The party began at noon right after church and would continue well in to the night.

TWENTY-THREE

The Crash

It happened almost overnight and with little warning. In October of 1929, the stock market crashed. The ripple effect of the collapse touched not only investors, but also every American family. In the 1920's, many had speculated that the U.S. economy was in an almost never-ending rise and the stock market was a popular investment vehicle. Reports of instant millionaires enticed people from the workingman to the wealthy to invest in the stock market. All hoped for an instant reward. Even though Nils and Linnea never thought of risking the little money they had in the stock market, the crash would, eventually, take a toll on them also.

The collapse of the market had completely traumatized the economy. Many banks were forced to close and the general population was afraid to spend money on anything but the basic necessities. As a consequence, most businesses suffered nation-wide. This included housing and construction, which slowly deteriorated Otto's business down to a trickle of contracts. He was forced to let many of his employees go but managed to hold on to Nils with a reduced staff. Although Nils still kept his job, there were many days during the week that he was without work.

With little money coming in each week and a mortgage to pay, a family decision was made to see if either Siri or Asta could find a job to help pay the bills and keep food on the table. There was a strong possibility that the girls would have to drop out of school if they found full-time work. Although they were disappointed at the prospect, both were more than willing to make the sacrifice to help support the family through a difficult time. They were not alone in their predicament. Many of their friends were in a similar situation.

Fortunately, both Asta and Siri quickly found part time work at the local grocery store while they continued to look for full-time jobs. For the moment, they managed to stay in school. The money they earned was kept in a large wooden bowl in the center of the kitchen table. Even Billy was eager and surprisingly able to help. He had become friends with Johnny Ellerson who lived a few doors down from the Vensbergs. Johnny, who worked as a caddy at the Oak Lawn

Country Club, encouraged Billy to apply for a job there. Billy, who was only eleven at the time, but tall for his age, persuaded the caddy master to put him on for a trial. He quickly picked up the routine, fell in love with the game and managed to make some handsome tips from the club members that appreciated his enthusiasm. Sometimes in the early evening when things were slow, the caddies were allowed to play a few holes. With only a few old clubs borrowed from the caddy master, Billy would take every opportunity to play. By the end of the summer, he had become addicted to the game and would often sneak out of the house through his bedroom window to play a few holes in the early morning before the club members arrived for first tee time. It wasn't long before he became quite an accomplished player for his young age. This was a talent that years later would save his life.

Over the next several months, it became apparent that Siri and Asta would have to find permanent work. Nils's hours were being cut more and more each week. He was able to pick up some extra work remodeling the Saint Cyprion Catholic Church but, unfortunately, it was not enough to cover all of the weekly expenses. When the situation seemed to get worse and food on the table was scarce, Nils would tell the story of his hard times growing up as a boy in Sweden.

"So you think we have it bad now?" he'd tell the family.

"When I was a little boy, I was one of twelve children and all we had to eat some days was one smoked herring and a potato. My father would hang the herring from the ceiling on a string and we'd take turns jumping up to lick the fish followed by a bite out of the potato. Then we would get back in line and do it all over again until both the smoked herring and potato were gone."

Only little Mickey believed the story with wide eyes. Even though Billy, Siri, and Asta knew the story was made up, it served the purpose of making light of a gloomy situation. Whenever it seemed everyone was a bit down, Nils would tell the same story over and over again and when he began with, "When I was a young boy we only had…" Everyone would groan as if to say, "not again." But then the groans were followed by a smile and the tension was broken.

Asta was the first to find full time employment at the Mars candy factory in Elmwood Park. The Mars Company was one of the few businesses that were able to insulate themselves from the economic downslide of the great depression. The head of the Company, Frank C. Mars, moved his company from Tacoma Washington to Minneapolis Minnesota in 1920. It was there that his sixteen-year-old son Forrest, suggested it would be a terrific idea if Mars could make a candy bar taste like a malted milk shake, a drink that was popular at the time and sold in soda fountains and drug stores across the country. It took three years to develop, but finally the Milky Way made its debut in 1923. Selling for five cents, the candy bar was a huge success and raised sales eight-fold. In 1929, Mars moved the company to a new production facility in Elmwood Park, Illinois where he could take better advantage of distribution routes. Quickly, the Snickers Bar (named after one of his horses) was introduced the next year and was followed by the Three Musketeers in 1932.

One of the unique attributes of the Mars Company was the culture in the work place. Their management style incorporated cross training and other distinctive approaches that were often copied by other companies. Quality was of primary importance, and the employees were expected to keep the production facilities in immaculate condition. The reward for self-sufficiency and productivity was a pay rate that was above average for the industry. The Mars family wanted to keep the work force intact and would frequently match or better any offers by competitors for the services of one of their employees. As a result, their turnover rate was extremely low.

It was a work ethic which was very familiar to Asta, and she quickly adjusted to her new job. She was meticulous about detail and it wasn't long before she was selected to hand-pack all of the sales samples and holiday gift arrangements. The only disadvantage of the full-time job, however, was it left little time for Asta to teach her regular evening bible study class at the church. Often, she would have to ask a friend to substitute for her, a situation that did not sit well with the pastor. He began to reprimand Asta every chance he could about how she was shirking her duties.

Dinnertime at the Vensberg's was a chance for everyone to catch up with each other about school, friends, their jobs and everything else that was important to them. When Asta mentioned to the family that the Reverend was pestering her about irregular attendance at Bible study, Nils immediately set down his fork. It didn't take much to set him off when it came to the church and its administration.

"He did what?" Nils asked with a face that was quickly turning crimson. "If it wasn't so late I would head down over to the church this instant to give him a piece of my mind. I'll just have to pay him a visit first thing tomorrow morning". That was the final word and an abrupt end to the dinner conversation. Asta was reassured.

Early next morning, the Reverend was startled by persistent knocking on the door. When he opened it, he was surprised to see Nils standing there. Nils didn't apologize for the unexpected visit and he began without hesitation.

"It seems you have an issue with Asta about her attend-dance as a volunteer teacher for the evening Bible class. In case you are not aware, Reverend, we are in the midst of some very difficult financial times and many families are struggling just to keep food on the table."

"Now Nils I don't think…" he interjected.

But Nils held up his hand to the Reverend and said, "Please do not interrupt me, I am not finished. In our case, Asta now has a full time job trying to help us pay the mortgage and other expenses just to keep our heads above water. I might remind you that her work as a bible study teacher is strictly voluntary and she cannot always be in attendance now because of her new job. She has never, however, and I repeat never, left the class without a teacher. She has always been able to find a substitute. Personally, I find it difficult to understand how a person in your position does not have more compassion and understanding for the plight of your church members. I'll thank you to leave the reprimands of my children to me in the future."

"Nils I am sorry you feel that way, but…"

The Reverend tried to explain and once again, Nils would have none of it.

"I think I am finished now. Good day Reverend" and with that, Nils turned around and walked out. He hadn't given the Reverend a chance to respond.

However, it wasn't the last time that the Reverend would anger Nils. A few weeks later he did it again—and it would be for the last time. Every Sunday morning there was always a particular point during the service when he would address the followers with announcements. On this particular Sunday, the announcement had to do with the dwindling amount of contributions to the offering. Each family had been supplied with offering envelopes and he knew exactly how much each family was contributing. This Sunday, he decided to call out the names of each family and tell the congregation how much they were contributing. Incredulous at the audacity and insensitivity of the Reverend, it was Linnea, surprisingly, who looked at Nils and said,

"I think we should leave."

Nils quickly responded, "I agree, tell the children we are leaving now." In silence the family rose up from their pew almost simultaneously and proceeded to leave the church while the Reverend continued to announce the names of each family and the amounts that they were contributing each week. It was the last time the Vensberg family set foot in this church.

Not long after, Siri found a full time job with the Illinois Bell Telephone Company as an operator. Although Illinois Bell had slowed down its growth during the depression, there still was a demand for female telephone operators. Both Siri and Asta had full time jobs now and the economic pressure on the family was relieved somewhat. They settled into a period of relative calm.

TWENTY-FOUR

A Trip to Mars

In the spring of 1933, one of Asta's co-workers told her of a notice posted on the bulletin board. It offered a job for a carpenter at the Mars factory. Her friend knew that Asta's father was a carpenter by trade and was having a difficult time finding steady work during these years of the Depression. Grateful, Asta could not wait to get home and discuss the possibilities over the evening dinner.

It was good news for everyone at the dinner table, especially Nils, who was becoming weary of the insecurity he felt not having a steady job. Linnea was even more relieved, as she knew how much Nils enjoyed working at his trade and how disappointed he had been for such a long time in not finding full-time employment. What Asta knew, but was not going to mention at the table, was the Mars policy of nepotism. Company rules stated that immediate family members could not work together. She was more than happy to give up her position so her father could work full time again, but she held back in telling him about the rule. She knew she would have to quit if he got the job but didn't want to dampen the enthusiasm of the moment. She also knew her father would not go for the interview if it meant that she would lose her job.

The interview went very well the next day with a glowing letter of recommendation from Otto who was only too happy to help. He had felt awful that he could no longer give his good friend Nils full-time work. The supervisor explained to Nils that the job was his and he could start immediately but there was something he had to explain to both Nils and his daughter Asta. He called Asta into the interview room and explained the policy of nepotism at Mars to both of them.

"Nils", he began, "I have already had this conversation with Asta and she really wants you to have this job. She has a full understanding of our company policy, which doesn't allow immediate family members to work together at Mars. Asta has told me she will step down from her job to make sure you have a full time position with us. She has been an exceptional worker, but we have to follow company rules."

Nils turned to Asta and asked, "Asta are you sure that

this is what you want to do? I wish you had told me about this before."

"It's OK Papa, don't worry", she replied, "You will be making more money than I would and besides it will be easier for me to find another job".

Begrudgingly, Nils accepted the company offer knowing that it would be the best choice for the family. Asta was already on her way to collect her things and say goodbye to her fellow workers.

When Nils came home that evening a very worried Linnea greeted him. She tried to keep calm as she said, "It's nearly six and Asta has not come home yet. She left the house with you at 7.00 A.M. and I haven't seen her since. It's not like her to wander off without telling us."

Now Nils was getting concerned as well, "She did not seem upset at all when we met with the supervisor and he explained about the company policy of family members. I expected that she would collect her things, say goodbye to her fellow workers and come straight home. I have no idea where she might have gone."

No sooner had Nils finished his thoughts than in walked Siri and Asta.

"Where have you been Asta?" asked Nils. "Your mother and I have been worried sick."

"I am so sorry. I've had had a long but terrific day," Asta exclaimed. "When I left Mars it was still early in the morning and I walked down to Lake Street in Oak Park to see if I could find someone that was hiring. I went to Marshall Fields, Wiebolts and The Fair, but had no luck. I even asked in some of the smaller shops in the area but there was no work anywhere. By then it was getting late, so I started to walk back home.

On the way, I passed by the Illinois Bell office and decided to pay Siri a visit. I waited until her break and told her of my day trying to find work and she mentioned that one of the operators had to leave early a few days ago. Her mother was in the hospital and now she did not have anyone to take care of her eight-month old baby. While I was there, Siri asked her supervisor if the girl was coming back and mentioned I was looking for work. I must have been at the right place at the right time as the supervisor told Siri the girl would not be returning and if I wanted the position I could start tomorrow and train with Siri. So there you go. See Papa, I told you I would find work."

"That's great Asta, just don't scare us like that ever again. Now let's all sit down for dinner. It's been a very good day," said a much-relieved Nils.

As was the custom many nights after dinner, Nils would

break out his violin to play for everyone. And Mickey, who was taught to play piano soon after they moved into the big house, would play "Sleep in the Deep" to accompany Billy while he sang. That was always followed by a quartet of Nils, Billy, Siri and Asta. It had been indeed a very good day and everyone enjoyed the evening. Their spirits were lifted. Linnea

Siri at Illinois Bell

treated herself to a glass of fig wine and smiled while she sat in her favorite living room chair and watched her family enjoy the evening.

The following day, with Billy and Mickey gone off to school and everyone else at work, Linnea headed next door to pay Mrs. P. a visit. She had not been feeling well of late and Linnea wanted to keep a close eye on her, as Mrs. P. was getting up in years and not moving about very well. She and Linnea had become very close friends over the years. This was unusual for Mrs. P., as she was something of a recluse not wanting to engage with many on the block. Her birthday was during the same week as Mickey's and so they made it a tradition to celebrate both birthdays on the same day each year. Linnea would make a coffee cake and Mrs. P. would bake a birthday cake for the three of them. Mrs. P. became something of an enigma on Hessing Street as the rumors persisted that she was part of the Guggenheim family on the East Coast. Although she would never mention much about her family, she did tell Linnea that she moved to Chicago to get away from her "east coast relatives." Linnea believed the rumors about Mrs. P., as every other month a chauffeured limousine, presumably with her brother inside, would come to her house and deliver food and money to make sure she was well taken care of. There was always more food than she could handle in the form of smoked hams, sausage, cheese and an assortment of chocolates. Mrs. P. would always give a generous portion of the food to the Vensberg family to enjoy.

When Linnea entered the home of Mrs. P. she found her lying in bed able to speak in only a very muted and weak voice. Normally, she was up early so Linnea was surprised to see her in such a weakened state.

"Are you not feeling well Mrs. P.?" Linnea asked.

"Oh I'm OK, just a bit weak today. I think I'll just take it easy and rest…and hope I'll be back on my feet tomorrow."

After her short visit—Linnea did not want to tire her friend out—she asked, "Is there anything I can get you before I leave? You need your rest Mrs. P so I think I'll be getting back home now."

Mrs. P., in a weak whisper, asked Linnea to "Just bring some bread and a glass of milk before you leave and sit it on the night stand next to my bed."

Linnea did as she was asked, said good-bye and told her that she would be in next morning to check up on her.

The girls and Linnea had always admired Mrs. P.'s beautiful diamond stud earrings that she wore every day. She was reluctant to say just where or how she got them, but was never too shy to tell Linnea that she was going to make damn sure her family was not going to get them when she died. She would swallow them if she had to!

The next morning when Linnea went over to check on Mrs. P. she knocked on the door but did not get a response. Concerned, she opened the door and found Mrs. P. still in bed apparently asleep. Linnea, in a hushed voice, asked if she was all right. Not getting an answer, she gently put her hand on Mrs. P.'s arm to nudge her. She was cold to the touch and Linnea knew immediately something was terribly wrong. It did not take long for Linnea to determine that Mrs. P. had passed away sometime during the night.

Before she turned to leave and tell Nils of the sad news, she noticed that the bread she left on the nightstand the day before was gone and the glass of milk was also empty. Stunned, she also could not help but notice that Mrs. P. was not wearing her diamond stud earrings. Linnea smiled and thought to herself, *Even in her weakened state, she knew she wasn't going to survive the night. Now I understand why she asked for bread and milk...she removed her earrings, rolled them into a ball of bread and swallowed them with the milk! Now they're safe...she's kept them out of the hands of her family!*

TWENTY-FIVE

"And all good things are yours"

On a cold Chicago afternoon in 1950, Nils and Linnea's family began to arrive for Christmas. First to arrive was Siri, with her husband Earl Kahle and their three children Judith, Jerry, and Jimmy—names affectionately pronounced by Linnea with her Swedish accent as Yudy, Yerry, and Yimmy. Everyone brought food—Siri's potato casserole was on the kitchen table next to Linnea's platter of Swedish meatballs.

Next to arrive was Asta with her husband, Irv Kossack and their two sons, Irvy and Larry. There were hugs and handshakes all around as Asta placed her Jell-O mold and rhubarb pie on the table. Earl and Irv, both of whom had played in the amateur leagues, were soon engaged in conversation about the Chicago White Sox' moves for the next baseball season.

Right behind Asta came Mickey, with her husband, Bill Sauter and their two children, Spence and Linnea. Mickey had made her favorite casserole and laid it next to the rest of the food. This display of delicious food plus the aroma of the freshly baked bread that Linnea had just pulled out of the oven, made everyone anxious to eat.

L to R: Mickey, Siri, Asta and John

The last to arrive was John (Billy) Vensberg with his wife, Genevieve, and daughter, Janice. Drafted into the Army in 1942, he returned home four years later. During his boot camp training, he had managed to play golf on Sundays with a borrowed set of clubs. At six foot two, he had the leverage to drive the ball a country mile and it wasn't long before word got out about how good he was. He regularly played par or better. By the end of boot camp, he was playing as a fourth with some of the officers who not only admired his game, but also enjoyed his engaging personality and good sense of humor. As a consequence, at the end of training camp Billy was sent directly to England where he taught golf to officers, gave exhibitions and occasionally played with the Army Gold Team. He never saw combat—the game he loved had been a lifesaver.

Linnea and Nils sat in a corner of their living room, each with a glass of fig wine and watched the grandchildren play as their parents engaged in lively conversation. Nils turned to Linnea, raised his glass and said to her with a wide smile, "Here's to us…it's been a tough journey but we've done a good job Linnea, a really good job."

TWENTY-SIX

On the Move Again

Nils loved his job at Mars. They were so impressed with his skills that, after only one year on the job, he was asked to do some repair work at the home of Frank Mars in River Forest.

The Mars family was extremely private. They rarely allowed photos and never made public appearances or issued any statements to the press. It was only after great scrutiny that they allowed someone to do any work on their home. They were not only impressed with the work that Nils did for them, but were comfortable that he would be discreet.

As the years went by, Nils repaired doors, made cabinets and shelves, created room additions, and remodeled a number of bathrooms. Over the next eighteen years, he spent more time at the Mars family homes than at the factory.

Nils and Linnea

In 1951, with their children settled, Linnea and Nils decided to retire. Although saddened by the announcement of his retirement, Mars presented Nils with a generous retirement package in appreciation of not only his contribution to the factory but also for his respect for the Mars family and their desire for privacy. In all the years that Nils did carpentry work at the Mars family homes he never would discuss what he saw or heard…even with his own family. With the money from Mars they bought a parcel of land in Miami where they planned to build yet another house. It was agreed by the family that Asta would stay in the home on Hessing Street with her family and pay Nils and Linnea a modest monthly rent that would help supplement their retirement income.

In the months prior to moving to Miami, Nils and Linnea were excitedly drawing up plans for their Florida home. Nils was approaching sixty-five but still determined to build yet another house on his own. It would be a small two bedroom one-story house with no basement—a construction plan that would be much easier for Nils to manage. They spent many nights together working out every detail just as they had done while planning the house on Hessing Street more than thirty

**Nils and Linnea digging the foundation for
their retirement home in Florida.**

years earlier. Linnea, as before, was never short of ideas to improve the layout, especially when it came to the kitchen. After the plans were complete they set off for Florida again, only this time under more favorable circumstances.

Once again, with a minimum of help, Nils and Linnea managed to finish a new small home near Miami. Nils had the time now, and took great pleasure in building most of their furniture and making cabinets for the small kitchen and dining room.

As they settled in, Linnea found her place in the sun and Nils fell in love with deep-sea fishing. The beach and the warm weather were a constant source of joy. Occasionally, when Nils went off to go fishing, Linnea would escape to the famed Hialeah Park race track where she could enjoy the beautiful surroundings of the park, filled with hundreds of pink flamingos wading through the shallow ponds in the center of the race track. At the time, Hialeah Park was considered the most famous and well-attended racetracks in the country. It was pure joy for Linnea to once again watch the handsome thoroughbreds parading on the track with their jockeys dressed in colorful silks. She loved taking the bus to the Hialeah track. It was on one of those trips that she would meet a new friend, Adalyn Stevens.

That day, Linnea boarded the bus, paid her fare, and could not help but notice a sign "COLORED SEAT FROM REAR".

She remembered that she had first seen signs like this in Savannah, Georgia on their way with the children to Tampa. It was difficult for her to believe that this practice was still in place after so many years. Curiously, the bus was full, with even a few people standing in the aisle holding on to the railing. Not finding any seats in the front, Linnea pushed towards the back where she noticed a few seats left in the "colored section". Without hesitation, amid menacing looks from the "white" patrons, Linnea took a seat next to a tall woman with skin the color of honey, dressed in an immaculate starched pink uniform with *Casa Lu Motel* embroidered on the front pocket. Just as startled as everyone else on the bus, the woman looked at Linnea as if she had seen a ghost. Linnea was not bothered in the least, but seeing the discomfort in the woman's face she gave her a reassuring smile and said rather innocently, "Beautiful day we are having isn't it? I am Linnea and you are?"

The woman had never been confronted with a situation like this before and was not quite sure whether she should respond or not, for fear of some type of reprimand. After a long pause, however, she quietly answered her, "My name is Adalyn…Adalyn Stevens."

"Well Adalyn, it's very nice to meet you. I am headed for Hialeah Park and you?" Linnea replied without the slightest hint of apprehension.

Ever so slowly Adalyn became more comfortable with this audacious woman who had a strange accent and began to answer Linnea's questions with less and less trepidation. Over the next few stops, Linnea talked incessantly and was curious to learn all about Adalyn and her family. When it came to Adalyn's stop they said their good-byes and promised to continue their conversation if and when they should meet again on the bus. When the bus reached Linnea's stop she pushed towards the front and as she was stepping down to the curb the driver warned,

"Lady, if I was you, I wouldn't sit in the back of the bus again with the colored folk."

"Tack sa mycket", she answered in Swedish…and then in English so he would understand, "I'll take my chances." She never looked back.

Over the next several years Linnea would occasionally find Adalyn on the same bus. Adalyn would give Linnea a wave and a gleaming white smile, as Linnea would walk straight to the back of the bus to sit with her. By now Linnea was accustomed to the stares as she moved toward the back. Unperturbed, she would smile politely at each of them but at the same time think to herself, *shame on you, shame on you… shame on you,* as she passed by them one by one.

Linnea learned that Adalyn had emigrated from Jamaica with her husband and four children to the United States in 1947. Her husband had found work as a night watchman at the Casa Lu Motel; a short while after, he managed to find a job for Adalyn cleaning rooms at the same motel. She didn't see her husband much because of the strange hours but it did enable one or the other to be constantly with their four children. It was the only way they could both work and also take care of them properly. The arrangement was not the best, but they needed the two incomes to keep their heads above water. The motel was conveniently located near Hialeah Racetrack. It was also an easy drive from Miami Beach, which made it a hot spot for tourists. They rarely had an empty room, and Adalyn felt that they had, for the moment, some sense of job security.

Linnea's encounters with Adalyn were always an after dinner topic of conversation with Nils. The mere mention of segregation immediately reminded him of the time he had to explain this practice to Siri and Asta while on the train leaving Savannah.

"It was difficult to explain then as it is now, but it's even more difficult to explain why it still exists today. It's amazing what human beings will do to harm each other," he would say.

Linnea could not stop thinking about how similar her

circumstances had been to Adalyn's in many ways but with different results. Both were immigrants, both had four children and both had worked very hard to establish themselves as part of the American lifestyle that was supposed to be full of hope and reward. The startling difference was the result of their efforts to establish themselves as part of this society. Despite many setbacks along the way, Nils and Linnea were able to give their children an opportunity to live a comfortable middle class lifestyle and later they were able to reach a contented retirement in Miami. Adalyn and her husband had also worked very hard to create a better life for their family in America but it was doubtful, because of their color, if they would ever be able to achieve the level of success that Linnea and Nils enjoyed. It was a thought that constantly annoyed Linnea.

Linnea and her granddaughter, Linnea

Over the next several years, both Linnea and Nils settled happily into their retirement routine. During the hot summers in Miami they would travel to Chicago to visit with their children and grandchildren and in the winters their friends and relatives would come down to Miami to briefly escape the cold. Some years it would be Linnea's sister Frida and her husband John or Nils's sister Gerda and her husband Gustaf from Boston. Even Victor and his wife from Piper City managed a visit.

But one day, the unexpected happened…and their idyllic life came to a halt. In 1956, Nils, who was seventy, had a brain aneurysm that took his life.

Linnea was in shock. She had lost her best friend. For the first time in her life she was completely disoriented and could not figure out what to do next. She had been strong and resolute in overcoming tuberculosis while living in a tent out in the wilderness. She had faced head on the throws of the great depression and even gave birth to little Mickey in her bedroom…but this was something that completely threw her off base.

It was a couple of days before she was able to collect herself and focus on what to do next. In her grief, she decided to move on and began to fill the trunk—the same one that had been baby Mickey's bed—with her belongings. She had a plan now. She wrote her home address on a piece of paper, wrapped her spare house key in it and placed it in her pocketbook. When she finished her packing she headed out the door to take one last ride on the bus to Hialeah Park.

It was a hot day and Linnea looked forward to the cool sea breeze. When she boarded the bus, she spotted Adalyn. Linnea smiled and waved as she pushed ahead to the back of the bus and sat down in the empty seat next to her.

"Hello, how are you," Linnea asked, "and how are your children…all off to school?" Linnea knew how hard it was for Adayln to get her four children off to school so that she could take the long bus ride to Hialeah, where she cleaned the rooms of the rich tourists staying at Casa Lu Motel.

"Oh they are a fine bunch but such a handful," declared Adayln in her lilting Jamaican accent. I just wish I didn't have to get them up with the crow of the rooster so I could make this bus. I am so weary…by the time I get home, I don't have much time to find out what they've been up to or even have a decent conversation with my husband! He and I are like ships passing in the night."

Linnea loved hearing her talk…her British accent was so clear, rhythmic and easy to understand. Conversation with Adayln was like music compared to the monotone of midwestern speech. She was sad to hear that Adalyn had to work so hard to keep her family in food. It made her even more resolute about the decision she had made; one that had prompted her to take the bus in hopes of meeting her again.

Then Linnea turned to Adalyn and began to explain the

sad recent events, "Adalyn I am afraid I have some terrible news. Two days ago Nils had a stroke and passed away. My oldest daughter is flying down today to help me make the arrangements to send the body back to Chicago for the funeral."

Adalyn was shocked to hear the news and took a chance …she put her hand on Linnea's and gave it a squeeze. It was a gesture that she hoped no one would notice.

Linnea was touched by her brave move on a crowded bus, but then realized she had to hurry with what she came to do before they had to go their separate ways. She reached in her pocketbook, took out her extra house key wrapped in the note she had written only hours ago, and gave it to Adayln. "Here is the key to my house. It's small but a lot closer to the beach and your work. I'm leaving Tuesday and won't be back… please take it and live in it with joy. The address is on this piece of paper. I'll write to you once I get settled in Chicago with instructions on how to transfer the house to your name. My daughter will figure out what to do".

Adayln started to protest but the bus stopped. Linnea gave her a hug and quickly got off. Waving from the curb Linnea thought, *it's time the neighborhood got a little more interesting.* True to her spirit, Linnea had made what she thought was a small gesture to help end the segregation of neighborhoods that was so prevalent at the time.

Later, on the move, she visited friends, and finally ended up living with Mickey and her family on the outskirts of Chicago. Sixteen years later, in the hospital, in pain and crippled with arthritis, she decided it was enough and stopped eating. In June of 1973, Linnea died at the age of eighty-six. She was laid to rest next to her husband Nils in the Elmwood Park Cemetery just across the railroad tracks from their home on Hessing Street.

Fear less, hope more; eat less, chew more; whine less, breathe more; talk less, say more; hate less, love more; and all good things are yours.

Swedish Proverb

* 9 7 9 8 8 6 9 3 5 9 9 7 1 *